Leadership
as a
Lifestyle

The Path to Personal Integrity
and Positive Influence

John Hawkins

Executive
Excellence
Publishing

For permission requests, contact the publisher at:

Executive Excellence Publishing
1366 East 1120 South
Provo, UT 84606
Phone: 1-801-375-4060
Toll Free: 1-800-304-9782
Fax: 1-801-377-5960
www.eep.com

For Executive Excellence books, magazines and other products, contact Executive Excellence directly. Call 1-800-304-9782, fax 1-801-377-5960, or visit our website at www.eep.com.

Printed in the United States

Printed by Publishers Press

10 9 8 7 6 5 4 3 2 1

Library of Congress Cataloging-in-Publication Data

Hawkins, John L., 1954-
  Leadership as a lifestyle : the path to personal integrity and positive influence / John L. Hawkins.
    p. cm.
Includes bibliographical references.
  ISBN 1-930771-12-6
  1. Leadership. 2. Leadership—Moral and ethical aspects. I. Title.
  HM1261 .H39 2001
  303.3'4—dc21
                          2001004667

Acknowledgements

This book is written with great appreciation to the following people:

The mentors who have taught and helped me along the way.
The hundreds of college students who have learned the lessons of lifestyle leadership.
Ann B. Sowers who has loved me and believed in me since the day that she brought me into this life.
Harold B. Bullock who has taught me by word and example how to be the man that I am called to be.
The Board of Directors of Leadership Edge Incorporated who have sacrificed in order to participate in raising up lifestyle leaders for the future.

This book is dedicated with loving appreciation to my wife Janet and our three children Laura, Gary and Will. It has been in our family that I have learned my most practical and important lessons on being a lifestyle leader.

Table of Contents

1 · One Reality

The Expense Report Syndrome

Seething over her seat assignment, Sarah collapsed into center seat 20B. No first-class upgrades, no aisle coach seats, and no approaching end to this exasperating day. It would be after midnight before she would finally rest in a hotel room in Cleveland.

As the jet lumbered down the runway, she wondered about her life. Her husband, Mike, and their teenagers, Matt and Amber, were the most precious parts of her life. Were her career and salary really worth the time she spent away from them? She always dreaded these monthly Chicago-Cleveland-Boston trips, but her boss had made it clear that they were non-negotiable. Sarah also knew that her next promotion would involve even more travel.

Reaching for her notebook computer, she wondered how Mike's day had gone. His small chain of garden supply stores was constantly challenged by the likes of Home Depot and Wal-Mart. The pressure seemed to be taking its toll. In fact, Mike told her recently that he felt like part of him had been destroyed over the last year. They both dreamed of taking a week or two vacation with just each other, but it didn't look possible anytime soon. Besides, how could they be gone that long from Matt and Amber?

Pushing through the clouds and the turbulence, the plane sailed onward. Today was Matt's quarterfinal soccer game. Sarah was so proud of him, both on and off the soccer field. His impish smile and quick rapport made him a "people magnet." He would only be at home two more years before leaving for college—possibly West Point. Mike and Sarah both believed that significant parenting still needed to be done before Matt would be ready to transition out of their home. And then there was Amber—precious, impressionable, over-achieving Amber. Sarah was convinced that Amber really needed her to be home more. In some ways, they were very much alike, but their interactions were often volatile. Sarah sometimes wondered if she knew anything at all about raising a daughter. She believed that parenting, preparing the next generation, was part of her "calling," or highest aim in life. How could she be so unprepared for the most important job she would ever have?

Sarah finished her pretzels and Diet Coke and absent-mindedly dusted off her hands. She knew she should start entering her expense report into her computer, but she just couldn't shake her introspective mood. Maybe she was eroding in the same way as Mike. She was convinced that her influence in her fam-

ily, church, and the community arts council was declining. These three spheres of influence and her job were her only major commitments. In each area she felt a sense of "calling," as if contributions in these areas were part of her ultimate purpose in life. They were all important, and she had to be successful in each! "It's all important, and it's all got to work," she desperately whispered to herself.

As Sarah finally began keying in her expenses, she grimly compared her life to the spreadsheet. Her life was made up of separate but interconnected little boxes or cells, too. She simply didn't have enough resources to go around, and the data in the cells of life kept running together.

Life Does Not Fit in Compartments

Compartmentalization is one of the most misguided approaches to life management. This strategy attempts to manage the maddening demands of multiple commitments by mentally separating each commitment into a self-contained, disconnected little box. Those who take this approach eventually realize that the walls of their compartments are paper-thin, with osmosis and reverse osmosis occurring constantly between the boxes. In other words, this approach does not hold water—it leaks.

Life is all about people, and people just do not fit into boxes very well. The commitments you make in your various spheres of influence are not to projects or institutions, but to people. When you attempt to compartmentalize your life, you prove how little you understand about life and the people in it. If you attempt to "manage" the boxes of your life, you quickly realize that the people in those boxes think very negatively about being shuffled around for you to maintain a mystical state of balance.

Furthermore, people with compartmentalized lives often begin to take on multiple personalities due to the alien nature of living life in little boxes. Who they are in the job box is different than who they are in the family box, which is different than who they are in their other boxes. Compartmentalization thereby results in life chaos rather than life management.

There are three common approaches to compartmentalization:

- Public and Private
- Career and Family
- Secular and Spiritual

The following sections address each of these misguided attempts to "divide and conquer."

Public and Private

"What a leader does in private is no one else's business." At times, this statement seems to be the one "moral" absolute of the political system. In fact, politics provides a perfect example of public and private compartmentalization, which proposes that public and private spheres are separate boxes in which different, and even conflicting, moral behavior applies. This belief trivializes personal morality into self-serving posturing

based on circumstance rather than conscientious, consistent alignment.

Political advisor Dick Morris proves it is impossible to manage life by separating public and private morality. Through his ongoing involvement with a prostitute, Morris betrayed both President Clinton, whom he served as advisor, and more importantly his wife, Eileen McGann. When called to account for his private actions by the *Star* gossip tabloid, Morris said he "knew instantly that everything was over and nothing would ever be the same."[1]

Morris' choice of words is revealing. When the press exposed the hidden part of his private life to the public light of day, Morris felt that *everything* was over and that *nothing* would ever be the same. This once respected and feared political guru came to see the stark reality that the walls separating the compartments of his life were exceedingly thin and permeable.

Career and Family

One of the greatest lessons to learn from the generation of those in their mid-twenties to late thirties (often called "Generation X"), and now the Generation Y (those born since 1984), is that the misguided compartmentalized notion of "quality time" does not work. These generations spearheaded our entry into the era of two-career families, acquisition for acquisition's sake, and latchkey kids. But Baby Boomer parents who play the "we can have it all" game too often crash into the wall of their bitter, shuffled, and half-parented children. Unfortunately, when parents recognize the problems their "have it all" attitudes often cause, it is often too late to repair the damage their abandonment has inflicted upon their children.

Every major career commitment you make either directly or indirectly affects your commitment to your spouse and children. The notion that you can consistently spend 60 to 80 hours per week in your career, and then go home with the energy and perspective needed to provide "quality time" is ludicrous. Similarly, it is ridiculous to think that the moral persona one puts forward at work can be substantively different from the moral example you want to build in your children.

The compartments of career and family constantly overlap one another, as Sarah at the beginning of this chapter demonstrated. This overlap forces us to admit that managing the commitments we make is nothing at all like filling in the separate cells of an expense report. Expense reports quantify the amounts spent in neat, separate categories. Unfortunately, managing your commitments is not quite that neat. Decisions in one sphere of influence affect our ability to fulfill commitments in all other spheres of influence.

The conflict between career and family commitments shakes us to the core of our values. Most spouses and parents really want to be invested in their families. They also want a successful and fulfilling career that provides financial security and enjoyable rewards. Many times attaining the universal dream of great family, great career, and great possessions proves to be a great nightmare of confused priorities, broken commitments, and fractured relationships. The most important question for us to ask is not some variation of "can we have it all?," but "what is my purpose?" As we come to clarity on a central life purpose, we gain perspective from which to manage our conflicting commitments.

Secular and Spiritual

The belief that religious and "practical" truth are of different substance and value is widely held in our society. Many believe that religious truth is important, but segregate it into its own sphere. Americans often accept religious truth only as it is personalized and exemplified in religious contexts. Many think that religious beliefs should be suspended when in a secular context and making secular decisions. Thus in the secular realm, such as the workplace, we expect spiritual truth to yield to practical truth.

This form of compartmentalization is most fascinating because it moves beyond compartmentalizing people and commitments and attempts to put God in a box. In this way of thinking, we roll God out of His box in so-called spiritual contexts, heed His sage wisdom, and then roll Him back into the box as we move into the secular world. This strange methodology reminds us of the old adage that in the beginning God made man in His own image, and ever since man has been attempting to return the favor!

This secular versus spiritual construct especially does not fit the Christian's understanding of God as put forward in the Bible. The Christian doctrine of God's sovereignty indicates that God directs all of humanity's actions to accomplish certain ends. Central to this belief is the idea that God is present in, and works His purposes through, all of reality. It is clear that this doctrine does not fit with the notion that religious truth is somehow subject to "practical" truth.

Furthermore, Christian doctrine teaches that God is the author of all truth. In other words, all truth is God's truth. This doctrine directly conflicts with our modern notion that secular truth comes before and is more compelling than religious truth in secular contexts. Moreover, because all truth is God's truth, the categories of secular and spiritual have no meaning. It is illogical to imagine that God is somehow unaware of our concepts of secular truth, or that He maintains two file cabinets in which He separates religious truth from secular truth.

This artificial division of truth into secular and religious categories leaves individuals disconnected from significant facets of reality—facets with which we need to connect to make balanced, wise decisions. In our workplace, we feel pressed to deny the reality, wisdom, and activity of the sovereign God that we worship privately. At our place of worship, we feel pressed to limit the scope of our worship to the work of God in so-called spiritual arenas, missing the instruction that we can receive by considering God's work throughout all creation.

The ineffective effort of managing life's commitments by compartmentalization is a futile endeavor that fails altogether over time. Life does not fit into boxes. More specifically, people do not fit into boxes, and God certainly does not fit into a box. The failure of compartmentalization leaves each stressed-out, overwhelmed individual with the challenge of building a unified life that communicates a consistent message.

A Unified Life and a Consistent Message
Human "Doers" or Human "Beings"?

As often observed, people are much more comfortable with "doing" than they are with "being." In fact, at times people seem to be human doers rather than human beings! The gnawing belief that "doing" defines one's value, whereas merely "being" just takes up space hovers over us all. The longing to establish our value based solely upon our accomplishments compels us to attempt life-management approaches that focus primarily on our roles rather than on our purposes.

The aversion to considering our purpose and then using it as a guide for our actions greatly minimizes the positive influence we can have in the lives of others. The depth of our influence with others is not primarily dependent upon the roles we play or positions we hold. The people we have become and the purposes we are fulfilling truly determine the depth of our influence with others. It is my belief that in its essence, leadership is a *lifestyle*, not a position. Solid, sustained leadership flows primarily out of who we are, not out of what position we hold.

Leadership positions do provide some tools of authority, such as resources and the ability to discipline. Yet in the lean, globally competitive corporations and organizations that dominate our world, the stretched resources and limited control of most managers exert little sustained influence over constituents.

It is the character, competence, and commitment of a leader that sustains and validates their leadership. These three foundational elements must be aligned with the moral beliefs and principles at the heart of the leader. A leader exerts influence with integrity only to the degree that this alignment is realized. When your character, competence, and commitment are not aligned with your moral beliefs and principles, your influence is compromised.

As we assume the roles of spouse, parent, boss, and citizen, our greatest influence will not result from the title that we hold. Rather, our progress in becoming persons of character, competence, and commitment will determine our influence and effectiveness. No matter the roles you are given to fulfill in life, your success will begin with the person you have become and the life purpose you are fulfilling.

Called to a Purpose

Most of us suspect that we have been called to be honorable and achieve something significant. When we say of others that they have wasted their lives or failed to go after a great opportunity, we are indicating that they "ought" to have been better or to have done more. As sophisticated members of the new millennium, we hesitate to specify what authority is behind this sense of "oughtness." Therefore, our sense of calling remains for most of us a suspicion rather than a certainty.

To have positive, on-going influence throughout the course of your life, you must gain greater certainty about this call to honor and significance. Working out your calling gives you the basis for honorable and significant interpersonal influence in the lives of others. You cannot help to establish in the lives of others that which is nonexistent in yourself. In other words, the quality of your influence cannot exceed the quality of your life.

And yet moving through life in the quest of becoming honorable and accomplishing significant actions misses the primary point of calling altogether. If you believe you have a personal call to honor and significance, you should logically move toward understanding the caller before pursuing the calling. If the call to honor and significance is a manifestation only of your conscience, then you must admit you are alone in the quest for honor and significance. If your calling comes from God, then you realize that the strength and guidance necessary for the pursuit of honor and significance come not only from within, but also from beyond. This realization of God's hand in our life's journey is a wonderful gift, a light on the long path of life's journey.

Looking back on the Expense Report Syndrome with Sarah, you see a woman who has mixed feelings about her real value and influence. In her marriage, family, and career, she wants to be respectable and to have significant impact. Yet she finds that her life and influence erode her emotionally. She feels an inner call but is uncertain how to translate the feeling into action. It is exceedingly important for her to know if this call is only from her conscience, or if there is a God beyond her that will empower and guide her. If it is God who calls, it makes all of the difference in the world. God's call comes from outside of us and is based on His character and purposes. The call that comes from our conscience comes from our own inner voice and is based on the core beliefs and virtues to which we ascribe. Conscience can be an important guiding source; it will never be an adequate substitute for God's call as we make substantive decisions.

The quest for understanding our purpose (what I am to be and to do) is a spiritual quest that leads us to the God who calls us. Any understanding of purpose that is detached from God is superficial and misguided.

Building a Life of Integrity

Leadership is comprised of character, competence, and commitment. These three elements of leadership must be aligned with your moral beliefs and ethical principles if you wish to lead with integrity. It is this kind of leadership—character, competence, and commitment that is coherent with moral beliefs and ethical principles—that is a lifestyle, not a position.

Those whose lives exemplify integrity understand that life is a seamless reality rather than a maze of disconnected compartments. Their aim is that within all their spheres of influence, they prove themselves to be persons whose lives communicate the same message. Whether on the job, with the family, or volunteering in the community, their influence is consistent and aligned with their moral beliefs and ethical principles. People who lead with integrity take their actions seriously. This is not to say they are rigid or morose, but they realize their integrity is sustained or diminished as a result of their speech and actions. In their actions and interactions with their families and coworkers, they aim for intentional communication and behavior. In so doing, they provide the kind of honesty and predictable steadfastness that is valued by those they influence.

Trustworthy Influence

A unified life that communicates a consistent message builds the trust of observers. Your ability to influence flows out of who you are and who you are becoming, which makes you credible to others. This also encourages those who interact with you to be receptive to your influence.

Managing life in a way that builds trustworthy influence does not come naturally. It requires focus, perspective, risk-taking, difficult decision-making, and constant realignment with your moral beliefs and ethical principles. As mentioned above, it also requires real clarity; you must truly understand the purpose to which you are called and the relationship that God wants with you. In other words, trustworthy influence requires a trustworthy foundation that does not change. By definition a foundation cannot exist within the structure that it supports; it must be outside and underneath the structure that it supports. Lifestyle leadership that communicates trustworthiness requires the leader to do the hard work of seeking and finding a solid, unchanging foundation. Trustworthy influence requires a trustworthy foundation.

It is a great cost to build a life that exerts trustworthy influence to others. The benefit of a life that influences and inspires others is also great. The two counterbalancing weights of personal cost and benefit to others define the decision you face when choosing to become a person of trustworthy influence. The satisfaction of knowing that one has chosen to live in such a way that his or her life has been honorable and truly significant is worth any cost.

The Key to Balanced Living
Faithfulness in All Spheres of Influence

When we reflect on our own lives, or on the lives of others such as Sarah balancing her expense report, we realize that one of the great longings of today is a sense of balance amongst the conflicting demands of our lives. In an attempt to manage all the facets of our lives, we frantically juggle our marriages, families, careers, and other spheres of influence at an ever-increasing speed. And therein lies the problem.

When we see life as a series of balls to juggle, balance is impossible. A master juggler is not working toward balance; he is simply coordinating the manipulation of the balls, but they are separate from him. We must recognize that attaining a life of balance cannot be achieved by manipulating people and things around us. Our goal is to manage ourselves in each area of influence so that we prove ourselves faithful in each sphere. We do this because all of our spheres of influence are important and our influence in each of them must work. This concept—"It's all important and it's all got to work"—is the beginning of building balance in our life.

"It's all important and it's all got to work" reminds us that no matter how loud one of our spheres of influence screams for our attention, we must fulfill our responsibilities in the other spheres as well. We do not have the option of giving 60 to 80 hours each week to our careers at the expense of our marriage and family. Neither do we have the option of cocooning in the nice safe world of our families and neglecting our commitments to our communities and churches. Leadership as a lifestyle demands that we engage and lead well in all of our spheres, not just in the one that is easiest, that complains the loudest, or that offers the greatest immediate rewards.

Balance Through Managing Conflicting Demands

Imagine a skilled snow skier swishing down a challenging mountain. Like the juggler we mentioned earlier, she is a picture of manipulation. She manipulates her body, primarily her weight, in order to successfully negotiate her trip down the mountain. In a matter of seconds, she shifts her weight from one side to the other and from the front of the skis to the back. She uses her muscles and weight to push harder on one edge of the skis and then to the other edge.

What would happen if the skier only shifted her weight to the left edge of the skis? Depending upon her speed and direction, she would either fall or stop. Either way, she won't arrive at the bottom of the mountain. Success on skis requires the constant shifting of weight and strength in order to master the irregularities of the slope.

The constant manipulation of weight and force by a snow skier is a great picture of what leadership as a lifestyle is all about. The leader lives in the center of the circle of his various spheres of influence. He realizes that if he only involves himself in one of the spheres, his neglect of the others will ensure his ultimate failure. He knows that success requires constantly balancing the need for his involvement, weight and force in all the spheres of influence. It is through managing the conflicting demands for his involvement that he actually comes to know balance.

The truth that balance comes from managing conflicting demands runs contrary to many people's thinking. Many think that balance is a constant state that comes from minimal involvement in only one or two spheres of influence. This theory looks great on paper, but it ends about there. The realities of life usually kick in and make this minimalist approach impossible; the minimum wage entry-level job leads to either a promotion with greater responsibilities or to termination with no pay, the carefree newly-wed couple gets pregnant with twins, or a just-retired executive finds himself responsible for a parent with Alzheimer's. Life simply has a way of complicating even the simplest of best-made plans.

The reality of adult living is that life becomes more complex and generates more spheres of influence. The degree of balance you find in this life comes from managing the conflicting demands of these evolving responsibilities. Balance exists in the managed tension of the weight of the conflicting demands, not in neglecting or abandoning those demands.

Patience, Courage, and Endurance

Those who practice leadership as a lifestyle realize their efforts are never perfect. The tyranny of urgency seduces us to neglect the important. Our efforts to be diligent in all spheres of influence can result in frustration, weariness, and failure, rather than the positive impact we desire. The challenge of being faithful in all spheres of influence drives us to recognize our need for transcendent help and grace from God. None of us have within our own hearts and minds all that is needed for affecting lifestyle leadership. Leadership as a lifestyle is not about building our ego, but about providing honorable and significant influence in all the spheres in which we are involved.

Three traits help lifestyle leaders' efforts succeed. You must have patience to grow as a leader, for results come over time. You need courage to make hard choices in the midst of demands from all sides. Finally, you must demonstrate endurance that stands up under the strain of conflicting demands and wrestles to find balance. These three traits sustain the leader and give perspective in the challenging times that all leaders face.

Wrestling with Living in One Reality
Inner Reflection and Honesty

This chapter delineates that life is one continuous reality, not segmented compartments or spinning balls to juggle. The concept that our life is one interconnected reality should force us toward inner reflection. Facing the reality of how our influence permeates all spheres of life takes time and can be painful. Being honest with ourselves in terms of the quality of our being, deeds, honor and significant accomplishments is not easy and must not be done superficially.

For those of us who pursue leadership as a lifestyle, there is the constant awareness of being in six feet over your head, with arms and legs sticking out all over the place. Life involves a lot of inner wrestling with the ever-present demands for our time and effort. The starting point for this wrestling is inner reflection and honesty. We need inner reflection that guides us in seeing all of our spheres of influence, not just the ones that scream the loudest or that most build our egos. Honesty is needed to confront those spheres of influence that we have either abandoned or that we have allowed to consume us. Inner reflection and honesty provide us with clearer understanding of the reality of our spheres of influence and the state of our leadership in those spheres.

A Network of Mentors, Coaches, and Sages

Becoming a lifestyle leader takes time and a commitment to learn. You can grasp some aspects of lifestyle leadership through trial and error. As you attempt to exert balanced influence, you can learn from both your successes and failures. This learning is invaluable and nonnegotiable.

There are also books and training programs that can help with lifestyle leadership development. Authors such as Stephen Covey and Ken

Blanchard provide insights for lifestyle leaders-in-the-making. The concepts put forward in Covey's *Principle-Centered Leadership* and Blanchard's *Gung Ho* can be very helpful.[2] The "Character First" training can also provide practical insights.[3]

Learning from the experiences and practices of others is perhaps the most often untapped resource for developing lifestyle leaders. A network of mentors, coaches, and sages from whom you can learn and receive encouragement will guide and direct you on your path to lifestyle leadership. Learning from others can speed your development process and bring clarity.

Building this network begins with reflection. Do you know someone who provides balanced influence in their various realms of responsibility? Initially, only one or two people may come to mind. As you learn from those people, the names and experiences of others will surface. You also want to build your network of associates who are also working toward becoming lifestyle leaders. The mutual encouragement, learning, and support that comes from friends is invaluable in providing perspective, guidance and modeling needed for our further development as lifestyle leaders.

Lifestyle leadership requires lifetime learning. The mentors, coaches, and sages that you find along the way will greatly facilitate the learning process. In learning to be a balanced leader, you don't want to wrestle alone. Grab the opportunities to learn and grow with others.

The Need for Transcendence

I hope that no one will interpret this strictly as a self-help book. My life is too much like Sarah's for me to believe that I can "self-help" my way into balanced influence that is both honorable and significant. The self-help mentality believes that if we know what to do, know how to do it, and empower our intrinsic motivation, we can succeed. I believe that from a broad, long-term perspective, this mentality is deficient.

I believe that within us all is a common brokenness to our humanity. Even when we know what to do, know how to do it, and believe that we ought to do it, many times we still don't. This reality sustains the diet-product industry. Each year more products are sold, and yet each year our population puts on more pounds. Diet plans tell us what to do, how to do it, and attempt to motivate us. However, what we choose to do when we smell the double-cheese pepperoni pizza is crucial. Our knowledge, ability, and motivation often capitulate when temptation meets motivation.

To be the leaders we must be in our marriages, families, and careers, we need the strength, grace, truth, forgiveness, and encouragement that comes from beyond ourselves. We cannot find these things in their fullness either within or around us. I believe that the adventure of becoming a lifestyle leader is simultaneously an adventure in coming to know and experience the God who calls us to be persons of influence.

2 · In Essence, Leadership Is a Lifestyle

The Myth of Leadership as a Position

Mark was furious. Why wouldn't Chris and Cindy do their jobs the right way—the way he wanted it done? No matter how many times he told them, no matter how many times he chewed them out and threatened to fire them, they still just couldn't get it right.

As director of Human Resources, you would think that Chris would know how to train people to stay in line with company policy. And yet their employees always wanted to get around policy—requests for telecommuting and flexible hours were constant. Mark had told Chris a hundred times that the company's greatest challenge was its loss of employee control.

In Mark's mind, Cindy was even more incompetent than Chris was. He hired her to be a basic "bean counter" and "number cruncher," and he had expected her to provide simple reports that spelled out the company's finances. But every month she had a new chart or analysis that was more confusing than the last. Why couldn't she just do the standard reports familiar to Mark? On top of that problem, Cindy had a habit of sharing the company's profit information with subordinates, which really sent Mark into a rage. The company's profitability was no one's business but the senior officers and stockholders.

As Mark sat in his office fuming over his latest confrontations with Chris and Cindy, he wondered what had happened to his influence. He used to be revered and feared in the company for his innate ability to get people to jump through his hoops. People stayed in their cubicles, got their work done, and went home glad to have a job. They did their work his way. Now it seemed like every chain of control he had was snapping. What had gone wrong with his workforce?

But Mark knew his problems weren't just at work. He felt as out of control with his wife and kids as he did with his employees. When he had married Mary, he thought she would be a traditional wife and mother. But when the kids had gone to school, she took a part-time job as a receptionist at a nearby real estate company. She claimed she needed adult interaction and some sense of accomplishment in her life.

Now, four years later, she was the top agent in the office with a work schedule that allowed her to be home in the afternoons when the kids get home from school. Her life seemed to move forward just fine without his involvement or input. Their communication focused on scheduling rides for the kids and investments for their retirement. Neither gave or required much from the other. Their careers and kids camouflaged their marital disconnection.

As Mark saw it, leadership was a lot easier in his father's day. Back then, everyone knew their place and understood the pecking order. Boy, were those days over! Now, he led employees who wouldn't follow, had married someone who could get along without him, and had kids that seemed to hate to see him come home. As a boss, a husband, and a father, he holds the positions of leadership, but doesn't hold the hearts and commitment of those he leads.

The Erosion of Positional Leadership
Breakdown of Authority and Hierarchy

Corporations spent the 1990s wrestling with the management phenomenon known as reengineering. More formally known as business process reengineering, the proponents of this movement claimed that by rethinking and restructuring the processes that employees use to complete the work of a company, the company could become more nimble, profitable, and globally competitive.

The reengineering movement proved to be a superficial solution to a complex human problem. At the time Michael Hammer, James Champy, and others put forward the original thinking behind business process reengineering, American companies languished due to a lack of competitiveness and profitability. Driven by money-hungry computer and consulting companies as well as frustrated managers, the movement devolved into a machine for drastic employee layoffs.

As Thomas Davenport states, "Reengineering treated the people inside companies as if they were just so many bits and bytes, interchangeable parts to be reengineered."[1] Though thorough in their approach to business processes, the proponents of reengineering were superficial in their understanding of the humans that ran the processes. They failed to consider the weight of matters such as loyalty, trust, and human dignity.

One thing the reengineering movement *did* accomplish was a substantive weakening of command-and-control leadership. As James Champy says it, "Managers in the new work models don't control any more. They're losing power. Power doesn't come from their position in the hierarchy any longer."[2] This reality rattled to the core many corporate leaders who were accustomed to managing people by jerking their chains.

The loss of control that comes from the weakening of corporate authority and the flattening of corporate hierarchies leaves many managers vulnerable and powerless. Authors Randall P. White, Philip Hodgson, and Stuart Crainer put it this way: "Strip many corporate leaders of their ability to control and their nakedness would be there for all to see."[3] As typified by Mark in our opening scenario, managers find themselves holding positions of leadership, but not the hearts and commitment of the people they manage.

Weakened authority and hierarchy has also occurred in American families. Families typified by television's *Leave It to Beaver* and *The Waltons* had a very clearly defined concept of authority and hierarchy. The phenomena of burgeoning divorce, latchkey children, "deadbeat" dads (and moms), feminism, dual-income families, and the powerful youth pop culture have greatly weakened the traditional roles of husband and wife, and father and mother. Television dramas and sit-coms that reflect the chaos and confused roles within today's families have replaced *The Waltons*.

Parents look at their children and teens and wonder if there is still a way to positively influence their development. Older children and teens look at their parents and wonder why they expect to have any control or influence in their lives. Reflecting the culture in which they have grown up, children now hire lawyers and divorce their parents. Husbands wonder if there is any real basis for them to be "head of the home." Wives wonder how they can wield enough power to control their husbands and children. As illustrated by Mark in the opening scenario, marriages quickly devolve into rapid-fire interactions over scheduling and finances in many families; who is in charge and how the family works and thrives together are questions with unclear answers.

Breakdown of Career Employment and Benefits

Today's leaders have also lost their ability to keep and motivate employees through promises of long-term employment and lush benefit packages. The competitiveness of the marketplace has forced companies and industries to undergo downsizing and mergers, which have destroyed any thought of career employment by one company. Today's college graduates enter the workforce realizing that they will most likely work for six to ten different companies throughout their working life, and very well may change the nature of their career several times.

The company career ladder has transformed into a moving sidewalk that moves employees from one company to another. Alongside the walkway, managers coax and tempt new workers like snake oil salesmen, promising futures that they cannot ensure. Their ability to retain, control, and motivate employees by career employment is no longer a reality.

Companies also find it very difficult to provide benefit packages that are good enough to motivate workers to stay. Managed health care has diminished many of the differences between employer-procured group plans and employee-procured individual policies. Nightmarish stories of retirement plans ravaged by the companies that established them have done little to build employees' confidence in their companies' commitments to secure a good retirement.

The loss of career employment and benefits as a mechanism by which managers can retain, control, and motivate employees leaves many managers empty-handed. Their position in the company leaves them with little ability to win their people's long-term following.

The Entrepreneurial Phenomenon

Generation X brought many significant and substantive changes to the American workplace. Members of this generation have also shaken many middle-aged and older managers to their company-policy boots. Those who lead today's twenty-somethings often come to the point of leadership meltdown. The telltale sign is when in absolute exasperation a manager wonders, "Why won't these twenty-somethings jump through our hoops?" These "hoops" may range from buying into the latest management fad adopted by the CEO to following procedures in the employee policy manual.

To the seasoned veterans of the organization, these rules and regulations are part of its tried-and-true standard operating procedures. To the twenty-something constituents, the hoops are the demeaning and meaningless instruments of personal control. The veterans see them as the way to move forward in the organization. The twenty-somethings see them as reasons to leave the organization.

Twenty-something Jennifer Singer describes it this way: "Sure, I tried the traditional route. But long before becoming eligible for a company watch, I found myself having a hard time adapting to the way corporate America operates… I thought it was silly that some superiors looked upon my leaving the office at exactly 5 p.m. as a lack of dedication. Most of all I couldn't understand why I had to report to an incompetent 'suit' simply because he didn't have 'assistant' before his title and I did."[4]

Rather than adapting to these conventions, Ms. Singer walked away from her employer and began her own public relations firm. In so doing, she joined the swelling ranks of twenty-somethings that have launched entrepreneurial endeavors. These men and women would rather succeed or fail based upon their own work and accomplishments, not because of their ability to jump through bureaucratic hoops.

The numbers of twenty-somethings interested in becoming entrepreneurs is significant. A random survey of 18 to 30-year-olds conducted by the International Directory of Young Entrepreneurs found that 60 percent of this age group wanted to own their own businesses within the next five years. The average number of students taking entrepreneurial courses at the University of Miami 20 years ago was 25; the average number today is 225 (Knight Ridder News Service). Paul Reynolds of Marquette University estimates that close to 5.6 million U.S. adults between the ages of 18 and 34 are currently attempting to start a business.[5]

The entrepreneurial spirit of this generation leaves many managers supervising employees who are looking for a good reason to quit and do their own venture. This reality weakens any hope the manager may have that their position will empower the retention, control, and motivation of their constituents.

"Rightsizing" That Downsizes Loyalty

Today's managers find themselves working in organizations that have been ravaged by the dehumanizing fads and competition of the 1990s. The euphemism "rightsizing" supposedly takes the sting out of the reality of "downsizing." Trends such as rightsizing have further eroded the possibility for organizational loyalty within the workplace. The massive layoffs and mergers of the 1990s have proven to this generation of workers that corporations cannot provide long-term employment or secure retirement.

Today's managers and executive leaders have a great need to build organizations that hold together and sustain profitability. Their leadership must be empowered by the loyalty and commitment of their people. The power of their positions is not enough to ensure loyalty and dedication to the job. The workforce has learned how to play the game—many employees do not plan to stay with any company for a long period of time. As soon as someone down the street or across the world pays a little bit more or provides a little bit better security for the future, the average worker is ready, willing, and able to jump ship.

When corporate downsizing occurs, the employees that remain can be an uncertain foundation for a manager to build upon. Many employees experience grief and disconnection due to the departure of some of their closest friends and associates. Along with this, they also may feel resentment toward management for the layoffs and the distress the changes have brought to all involved. Others live in fear that they will be next, or take days off to find their next job.

Considering the type of feelings and thoughts that downsizing "survivors" experience, it is easy to see how difficult it is for a manager to draw upon their loyalty to the corporation or its leaders. In many ways, the price that companies pay today for being competitive in the global marketplace is the erosion of employee commitment. Rightsizing the workforce also downsizes the reservoir of loyalty and relationships. This truth has left many managers with positions of authority, but with people who are too distracted or frustrated to follow.

A recent downsizing dismissal of a well-respected and highly productive team-leader gives an example of the resultant downsized loyalty. The team-leader was called to appear at a meeting at the beginning of the workday. His superiors told him that he was being dismissed immediately and would be given four months severance pay. His corporate-owned Palm Pilot was taken, his access to the corporate computer system was frozen and he was told that he could not return to his office nor tell his team-members goodbye. His boss told him that in a few days he would be escorted to his office by corporate security to remove his personal effects. This would occur either after his team left for the day or before they arrived in the morning.

Within a couple of hours of the employee's dismissal and departure from the corporate campus, his entire team found out what had happened. The team left their cubicles and met their former leader off site. Though he was unwilling to slander his former employer, his team returned to their jobs wondering who would be next, demoralized over why the company dismissed their honorable leader.

Imagine the difficulty the next manager will have in winning any loyalty at all from the team. Any commitment given by team members would most likely be momentary and self-serving. Successful leadership is much more than a title or position. A leader must establish trust at the heart of the relationship, especially with a team whose heart was ripped out.

From Control to Influence
You Can't Use What You Don't Have

From the *Bible* book of *Judges*, Samson is one of the most storied figures in Jewish antiquity. As the story is told, Samson was a man of inordinate physical strength who had a weakness for beautiful women. His strength was linked to a vow that he made to God, a vow that was symbolized by Samson's uncut hair. According to this vow, if Samson ever allowed his hair to be cut, his physical strength would vanish.

Unfortunately, Samson's deceptive lover, Delilah, learned of the secret link between his uncut hair and his strength, and was later bribed to deliver him to his enemies. She knew this would be possible only by cutting Samson's hair. As he slept in her arms, Delilah cut his hair, then signaled the enemy to seize him. Awakened by their entry, Samson stood to defend himself as he had done so many times in the past, not realizing that his strength was gone. He was quickly taken captive and led away.

Samson reminds us what today's leaders look like when they try to lead with a command-and-control style of leadership. They stand to lead, failing to realize that their power is gone. Their power, which was linked to the command of their position and their control of information and other resources, has evaporated. In the opening story, Mark was confronting this reality. In today's transient, disloyal, and temporary workplace, few desirable employees will stay around long enough to be commanded and controlled.

Parents realize the same truth in leading their families. Too often, teenagers see their family involvement merely as "pit stops." They hang around the house long enough to sleep, eat, get clean clothes, collect their allowance, and then they are gone. While they see their family as an inconvenient and often ineffective place to refuel, they see their friends as their real family. Parents who only exert a command-and-control leadership with their teenagers reap the result of shorter refueling stops. The parents' commands fall on the inattentive ears of teenagers rushing out the front door for their next social activity, school event, or athletic practice. The parents' control of resources falters as their kids enter the workplace world of flipping burgers at McDonald's or selling jeans at The Gap. Like Samson of old, today's parents stand to exert the command and control that they once had when their teenagers were children, only to realize that their strength has vanished.

Three Powers of Leadership

Every style of leadership has a source that empowers it. Ultimately, all power is validated or granted by a leader's constituents. It is a fallacy to look at successful leaders and talk about their powerful leadership. This analysis stops short of the reality that followers grant leadership. Religious martyrs have illustrated throughout history that even the most repressive leaders have no sway over those who are willing to die for their beliefs and principles.

The three power sources of leadership are:

Type	Method	Keyword
Coercion	Grab their throats	Control
Utilitarian	Grab their wallets	Economics
Life	Grab their hearts	Loyalty/Trust

Coercion, the lowest form of leadership, can be called the "big stick approach." Those who lead by coercion communicate with the following proposition: "I have a big stick. You can do the task that I need done. If you do the task, I will leave you alone. If you don't, you will suddenly feel the pain of this big stick across your back." Coercive leadership can be effective in the short-term, but it is counterproductive in the long-term.

Those who lead by coercion end up with constituents who either lack self-motivation or who are plotting an escape or takeover. Since the test of leadership is what the people do when the leader is absent, this approach to leadership is a failure in any long-term context. In recent history, the demise of the former Soviet Union provides a vivid illustration of the failure of coercive leadership.

Utilitarian leadership is the basic motivation of America's capitalistic workforce. Leaders using the utilitarian approach make the following proposition to their constituents: "I have money and need work to be done. You need money and you can do the work. If you do this work, I will give you this amount of money." This leadership approach has been effective in both short-term and long-term contexts in the past. However, today's marketplace has weakened the long-term effect of utilitarian-empowered leadership.

As described earlier, today's workforce is disloyal and temporary. If the only reason an employee stays is the amount he or she is being paid, as soon as someone else offers more, the employee quits. Strict utilitarian-empowered leadership has a tough time retaining long-term employees in today's competitive and global workforce. The materialistic lust for "a little bit more and a little bit better" drives employees from employer to employer.

Life-empowered leadership has the best chance of gaining long-term loyalty and commitment from constituents. This approach to leadership communicates to the constituents the following proposition: "These are my beliefs and values. They will guide my speech and actions as I lead you. As I model these beliefs and values, I expect that I will win the right to influence you in your own development and in our accomplishment of the goals and vision of our organization."

Life-empowered leaders keep their focus upon modeling the values and beliefs that they believe are essential to the success of the organization. They also focus on gaining influence with constituents concerning their development and their performance. The power of their leadership is not coercion or money, but the strength and goodness that emanates from them.

Tom Landry, former coach of the NFL Dallas Cowboys, was a life-empowered leader. During his 29 years with the Cowboys, his life-empowered leadership had positive personal impact, both on and off the field. His former quarterback Roger Staubach said of Landry's influence, "He was our rock, our hope, our inspiration. He was our coach. Probably there were some players that didn't love him, but they all respected him."[6] Landry's son, Tom, Jr., said of him, "Tom Landry was everything the world believed him to be. He was a man of virtue, of high moral character, a man whose talents and hard work propelled him to the top of his profession."[7]

At a time in which leaders are viewed with rampant cynicism, especially concerning their possession of moral authority, it is important for leaders to remember that their lives are the most powerful leadership tool they possess. It is true that utilitarian-empowered leadership and coercion-empowered leadership are appropriate in certain circumstances. But for effective long-term leadership, it will always be the life of the leader that sustains or destroys his or her leadership and draws loyal commitments from the people.

The Age of Mentors, Coaches, and Sages

To consider further the current need for leaders who model and influence, it is helpful to examine the burgeoning need for mentors, coaches, and sages in the business world. These three types of leaders rarely have the ability to exert any kind of command or control over their protégées. Usually this sort of relationship is a volunteer arrangement by both parties. Effective mentors, coaches, and sages lead from their wealth of experience, wisdom, and from who they are and what they have become; they lead by sharing, encouraging, and helping. When serving effectively, they provide wonderful and varied examples of life-empowered leadership.

Mentors and coaches live by the motto, "What you choose to become matters to me. How can I be of help?" A mentor tends to focus on general personal development and growth, whereas a coach generally focuses on personal development related to specific areas of job or goal performance. The protégée's development drives and defines the success of the relationship.

Ken Blanchard and Stephen Covey are two sages who serve as mentors to the masses. Through their books, tapes, and worldwide satellite-fed seminars, Blanchard and Covey share their expertise in a broadcast fashion. The influence of sages who broadcast their wisdom via the mass media is limited in that they do not work alongside a protégée in a local context. The business audiences that wait for each word that flows from the satellite feed pay top dollar to learn from the experiences and opinions of these and other sages.

The current popularity and demand for mentors, coaches, and sages suggest that Americans feel a strong need for personal assistance in order to succeed at life. In the maddening pace of the new millennium, spouses, parents, employees, and bosses realize that they need outside help in order to succeed. This often unspoken need for help provides significant insight to those who desire to lead.

Helping Others Succeed at Life

Leadership has always been a process of influence. Obviously, leadership involves influencing others to see the vision and to accomplish the mission of the larger group. But engaging constituents with the organizational vision and mission is only the starting point for the kind of influence that today's leaders need to exert. Those leaders who succeed also must be able to exert the kind of influence that helps people succeed at life, not at work only.

In this post command-and-control era, the workforce stays in a fluid state. Companies and leaders who have a reputation of benefiting their employees have the best chance of retaining loyal and productive workers. The leaders who commit to helping their employees succeed at life realize that what happens "off the clock" affects what happens "on the clock." They also realize that helping their employees includes, but also goes beyond, monetary gain.

These leaders realize that life-benefiting experiences such as the following can be realities in the workplace:
- Positive, meaningful relationships
- Stimulating, significant work
- Career and personal development
- Association with honorable people and accomplishments
- Transfers to new and interesting job assignments
- Support and encouragement for family life
- Support for personal financial security

Organizational leaders who have the reputation of benefiting their people in these ways demonstrate that their influence is not just about getting people to do work, but also helping people to succeed at life.

This kind of influential leadership is also very important in marriages and families. Spouses who conclude that their marriages are frustrating their own personal development and growth begin to look for a way out of marriage. Teenagers who think that their parents do not care about their happiness or success in life tune out or run away. Those who lead in their marriages and families must learn to facilitate their spouse's and children's development and become members of a team. This takes time, emotional energy, and a real commitment to bless and benefit, not just to command and control. As influential leaders prove themselves to be blessings and benefactors to their constituents, they establish one of the most precious ingredients to long-term, effective leadership—their credibility.

Lips Should Persuade and Lives Command
Influence Begins with Our Speech and Actions

"Our lips should persuade and our lives command." This proverb, attributed to Saint Athanasius of the early Christian Church, contains profound truth pertinent to leadership today. In this age, when moral authority and leadership seem to be antithetical terms, people continue to hope to find credible and effective leaders. Too often we have understood leadership as being about our lips commanding and our lives eroding. Leaders who aim for influential leadership that flows from who they are and not from the positions they hold understand that their credibility is always sustained or destroyed by their own speech and actions.

In the realm of speech and actions, a leader is never off the clock or off the record. The speech of the leader must consistently reflect the values and beliefs that are necessary for advancement of the organization and its people. The same is true for the leader's actions. The leader's credibility, like a stone wall, is built one word and one action at a time. The leader's use of humor, methods of verbal and nonverbal motivation, and personal demeanor must be consistently aligned with the organization's and his or her own values and beliefs.

As stated earlier, today's leaders must prove that they are committed to blessing and benefiting their people. The leader may claim to be committed to the hopes and aspirations of the people; speech and action prove the claims true or reveal them as a shameless sham. Time is always the context in which a leader's credibility is proven. Time is the acid test that determines the effectiveness and morality of any leader.

The Connecting Point of Influence—Credibility

The credibility of the leader serves as the bridge between their leadership and the constituents' commitment to follow. A leader and constituents can come together for substantive commitments to each other and the organization only to the degree that the leader's credibility is solid. If the leader's credibility is weak or lacking, the interchange between the leader and constituents tends to be fragile and superficial. Too much time and energy are expended on self-protection and verification rather than on joining together in significant accomplishment.

The relationship between the leader and constituent must eventually become a two-way interchange in which both parties prove themselves trustworthy. In this interchange it is the leader's responsibility to go first and to remain steadfast. With this methodology, the leader has great potential to attract and retain credible employees, employees who value honest lips and honorable actions and who believe that it is their responsibility to live accordingly. A two-way interchange of trust between leaders and followers is based upon a shared set of values that are commonly understood and practiced as well as a common commitment to accomplishing the team's mission and vision is also required. Confidence in the judgment and ability of those to be trusted is important for all long-term trust relationships. Leaders and team members prove their trustworthiness by putting forward these commitments. And as mentioned before, the leader must go first in proving her commitment. Great employees in like fashion follow their leader.

"Trust in a time of change is based on two things: predictability and capability."[8] This statement from Professor Jeanie Daniel Duck in the *Harvard Business Review* gives further insight into the credibility of leaders. Unpredictable leaders breed fearful or disengaged constituents. Incapable leaders breed unproductive or passive constituents. A leader's credibility is founded upon speech and actions, and it is sustained, especially in times of change, by predictability and capability.

Peter Drucker, Dean of American Management, says it well:

> The final requirement of effective leadership is to earn trust. Otherwise there won't be any followers—and the only definition of a leader is someone who has followers. To trust a leader, it is not necessary to like him. Nor is it necessary to agree with him. Trust is the conviction that the leader means what he says. It is a belief in something very old-fashioned, called "integrity." A leader's actions and a leader's professed beliefs must be congruent, or at least compatible. Effective leadership and again this is very old wisdom—is not based on being clever; it is based primarily on being consistent.[9]

Influential leaders who lead out of who they are exemplify what they want to help their constituents become. Their lives, as exhibited by their speech and actions, prove that they are committed to being persons who bless and benefit others. And in so doing, their constituents recognize that these leaders have fruitful lives that work.

The Final Result of Influence: Fruitful Lives

One of the cries of many people today is, "How can I get my life to work?" Americans of all backgrounds and circumstances wonder if there is a way to really have a meaningful life in the midst of the fast-paced and technologically driven culture by which we all too often feel controlled. Our own memories, favorite books, even reruns of television shows like *The Waltons* and *Little House on the Prairie* compel us to believe that once there was an approach to life that though challenging, was so much more meaningful.

During election years, our political leaders tell us that they know the way to the future or that they want to take us back to our country's former glory. Yet as their own lives are probed by endless media exposure, we too often come to realize that they are as overcome by the challenges of the age as are we. Their ability to rally us to move forward or to return to the past is undercut by their own misdirection and the stymied political processes that they propagate. They too often exemplify leaders whose own lives don't work.

What is true in politics is very often true in the workplace and the home. Executive leaders, as well as everyday moms and dads, feel obligated by their positions to communicate that they know the way. Yet at self-induced moments of crisis, they instead show that they have lost the way to building a life of meaning and service. Influential leaders are those who are committed to the continual learning processes of building a life and leading their constituents.

This kind of leader bears fruit for everyone's consumption. A leader's life is not focused solely on 401(k)s and climbing the corporate ladder. A leader sees life as a stewardship to others, and not as a means for self-indulgence and self-absorption. Leaders understand the words of the anonymous writer who said:

> *I shall pass through this world but once.*
> *Any good therefore that I can do or any*
> *kindness that I can show to any human being,*
> *Let me do it now.*
> *Let me not defer or neglect it for I shall not*
> *pass this way again.*

This understanding of the purpose of life builds both rich humility and a desire to live and lead boldly, without fear. These people see the leadership process as a way to help others accomplish significant, honorable goals that will bless and benefit all involved.

Two beliefs about life inspire influential leaders. First, the only real success in life involves positively influencing others. Second, one's ability to positively influence others is based upon the constant development of their character, competence, and commitment. These men and women see their lives as a mission to humbly and boldly bless and benefit those that God gives them to lead. In this mission, they pursue one of life's greatest adventures.

Using the Tools of Position
The Tools that Remain

Let's return to Mark at the beginning of this chapter. He typifies the leader who still understands leadership as a process of command and control. His frustration grows as he sees his commands ignored and his control evaporating. Mark is like a mechanic using primitive tools to repair a NASA space shuttle. The tools he is trying to use are doing more harm than good. He holds a leadership position, but he is failing as a leader.

What tools exist for leaders in today's organizations? In most instances, leaders still control the allocation of resources and the hiring and firing of personnel. They also have final say in areas such as direction setting and scheduling. Today's leaders certainly have some tools of control to use at their discretion. The problem with these tools is that they can do very little to build *loyalty* and *trust* with their constituents. Loyalty and trust form the glue that holds together organizations and families over the long haul. The tools that a leader uses to build loyalty and trust are primarily the tools of influence, not the tools of command and control.

The tool that ultimately remains for a leader to use to build loyalty and trust throughout the ranks is their own life. Mark thinks his problem at work has to do with compelling incompetent people to do work his way. His real problem is the lack of a foundation of loyalty and trust with Chris and Cindy from which they can work together on the corporation's needs. He realizes that his wife no longer needs his command-and-control approach to family leadership. She needs and wants true, life-empowered leadership. The truth is that he has ignored the opportunities over the years to build a marriage with her that produces loyalty and trust. He has lost the glue that could keep them together during the challenges of dual careers and raising children. His employees and family are leaving Mark behind because he clings to the old command-and-control method of leadership.

The scary and stark reality that Mark must face is that he is his own leadership problem. He holds the position, but does not hold the hearts and commitment of the people. As his life continues, his influence will only continue to decrease unless he changes his attitudes and methods. The most important tool that remains for Mark to use is the now dull instrument of his personal influence. He needs clear perspective and courage to realize this and to grow to be a person of influential leadership.

The Use and Misuse of the Tools of Position

People who hold leadership positions in today's organizations still have the ability to do such things as hire and fire, allocate resources, and set direction. It is important that these actions are used strategically and not capriciously or recklessly. Leaders can use the tools of their positions to help establish and sustain the influence that they want to affect.

Leaders often wrongly assume that their greatest leadership moments occur when they are delivering soul-stirring motivational speeches about the vision and mission of the organization. In reality, the leadership shown during hiring and firing, resource allocation, and goal setting speak a thousand times louder than their heart-stirring speeches. The motivational talks are merely words about the future; the leader's actions are the path toward the future. People are warmed by words, but convinced by actions.

The tools of positional leaders are of great importance to those who also want to become influential leaders. Those leaders who learn to use their positional tools to further establish their positive influence with their constituents grow in both leadership wisdom and balance. Their constituents are blessed with leadership that respects both the boundaries of the organization and the need of the constituents for meaningful accomplishment and development.

Influence and Position: Empowerment with Boundaries and Meaning

The following question is one of the true tests of long-term leadership: Over time, do the followers like who they are becoming as a result of their involvement with the leader and the organization that he or she is leading?

If the answer to this question is yes, the leader has reason to lean back in his or her chair with a fresh cup of coffee and savor the moment. If the answer is no, the leader should expect employees to leave soon or to remain under productive. If the employee does not see that their involvement with the leader and organization is affecting who they are becoming, the leader should consider what it would take to have that kind of influence in this constituent's life. If involvement with the organization doesn't help a constituent become the person he wants to become, that person's potential loyalty and commitment will diminish.

Bosses, spouses, and parents have a great opportunity to learn to be both positional leaders and influential leaders. As positional leaders, they can learn how to help their constituents accomplish great things within the boundaries of the organization. As influential leaders, they can leverage the power of their own words and actions to help their constituents learn how to make their own lives meaningful. In the opening story, Mark clearly typifies the leader who has failed to realize the power of influential leadership. How amazing it would be to see him slowly learn the lessons of leadership as a lifestyle. How equally wonderful it would be to see his associates Chris and Cindy flourish through their involvement with Mark, rather than hanging their heads and hiding out because of Mark's latest diatribe and demand for meaningless conformity. Imagine the hope that there is for his marriage and family if he were to reenter those relationships with a commitment to becoming a husband and father of personal influence.

Leadership as a lifestyle holds that the power of a leader's personal influence is more important than, but not a replacement of, the power of the leader's position. In today's culture, the tools of position alone prove to be increasingly ineffective over time. The tools of personal influence are essential and give direction as to how and when the tools of position should be used. Our families and our corporations desperately need leaders who lead out of what they have become, as well as out of the positions they hold. It will be these men and women who are privileged to experience the great adventure of leadership as a lifestyle.

3 · The Core of Sustained Influence

Character, Competence, and Commitment

As Rick and Cynthia left his office, Jerry wondered if either of them would still be with the company in six months. Both were failing miserably as leaders. Rick's team members got along great with each other, but their accomplishments were few and untimely. Cynthia's team got every project in on time, but was made up of high-achieving backstabbers and opportunists. While Rick's team slowed down the company, Cynthia's team poisoned it.

Jerry found Rick was the kind of guy everyone liked. But those who followed Rick quickly realized that while he was great to be with, following him was like walking in place. Jerry recognized that Rick was a role model ethically, but he was unskilled and disengaged when he needed to inspire high performance. Over time, high achievers assigned to Rick's team asked to move to other, more goal-oriented teams. The office had created a tongue-in-cheek motto for Rick and his long-term teammates: "nice people getting nicer."

Cynthia was completely different from Rick. The motto for her team was "accomplishment at any cost." On the surface, she looked like a very skilled leader. She regularly talked with her team about vision and goals. She was a hard worker and demanded the same from her team. Cynthia noticed the small steps her team made toward the realization of their vision and celebrated each accomplishment with them. For those who matched Cynthia's expectations of drive and achievement, her team was a great environment. However, Cynthia was vicious to any team members who failed to live up to her expectations.

Within two or three weeks of joining her team, Cynthia decided the new addition's worth. If the new member didn't make her high-achiever cut, Cynthia used any means possible to "encourage" that team member to leave. Malicious gossip and public humiliation were two of her most skilled "removal techniques." But there were other reasons for her team's high turnover rate. Some members did not like who they were becoming in this cut-throat atmosphere. Others adopted Cynthia's tactics and moved on to build their own regimes. Jerry recognized that the costs in "accomplishment at any cost" were too often the sacrifice of good people and the values of the company. In fact, the many accomplishments of Cynthia's team were extracting a huge cost from the rest of the company.

Jerry knew that neither Rick nor Cynthia could have much pride in their leadership. Rick led people to do too little, too late. Cynthia led people to exploit others for the sake of production goals. Jerry only wished he could develop the other's strengths, thus tempering their own glaring weaknesses. The company simply could not bear their negative impacts much longer.

Influence Emanates from Within
Leadership Weight Rather than Control

Weight or gravitas is much more important to influential leadership than control. Those who understand leadership as a lifestyle believe their success is much more dependent upon their example and abilities than upon their control and manipulation of others.

Influential corporate leaders realize that true long-term leadership comes through influence. A wise leader never gives up the control that their position affords them. Yet, if their leadership focuses primarily on exerting control, they lose their strongest employees and are plagued with a band of weak underachievers. Over the long term, one must learn to broaden and deepen their influence and loosen (but not release) their control.

Parents understand the same truth. Those parents who are influential leaders realize they often need to exert control in the short-term, but that true leadership of their children in the long-term must be through influence.

Influential leaders focus first on their development as a person and second on their development as a leader. Their hope is that over time, their example's force and leadership abilities will win them the right to influence their family and constituents toward strong values and strong achievement.

Winning the Right to Influence

In this chapter's opening story, Rick and Cynthia each possess one piece of the three-piece leadership puzzle. Rick has very strong personal character. His people trust him and respect him as a person. Cynthia can inspire motivated people to accomplish significant goals. As important as these strengths are to a leader, independent of each other, they prevent leaders from winning the right to influence their constituents. Rick does not have the leadership competencies to lead his people to high performance. Cynthia does not have the strength of character needed to lead her people to embrace high values while accomplishing their business goals.

As is true in all of nature, Rick and Cynthia can only reproduce in their constituents what they themselves are. Because of their developmental limitations, they are not able to influence their constituents to become people who live out high values and achieve high performance.

Influential parenting also requires personal character and leadership competence. Pre-adolescent parenting, which must effectively prepare kids for the teenage and young adult years, demonstrates these requirements very clearly. The parent's character must be strong during these often difficult years; the "do as I say, not as I do" doctrine simply does not work. The parents' ability to help their kids see and commit to an honorable life-vision must also be strong. Parental leadership that has disengaged from the children is simply not effective.

Your character and competence win or lose the right to positively influence the lives and performance of others. Influential leaders must remain ever vigilant to their continued development in these two areas. For truly effective leaders, "inbuilding" character and competence into their own lives precedes and sustains their influence on others' lives.

Inbuilding Precedes Influence

A grandmother once commented that she was amazed at how ill-prepared most of us are for parenting—one of life's most important leadership responsibilities. Through procreation you acquire the position of parent. However, succeeding as a parent is much more challenging than simply becoming one. Successful parenting requires, among other things, intentional growth in the values that lead to moral authority and in the competencies that lead to effective leadership. Good parenting requires ongoing growth.

Business leadership also requires ongoing growth. In the opening story, Rick and Cynthia appear to be stuck in their development as leaders. Most likely, both have developed to the extent that their personal comfort and awareness will allow. Further development will require focus, vulnerability, and humility—human attributes that do not fit well with personal comfort and unawareness. In the balance is the depth and breadth of their personal influence in the lives of those they lead. Will they pay the ongoing price to win the right to influence? This price involves the continual building of skills and attributes throughout the course of their lives. Only this constant growth will ensure their effectiveness as leaders of influence. For leaders, personal inbuilding always precedes positive organizational influence.

The inbuilding that must occur within influential leaders takes place in three areas: character, competence, **and** commitment. These three areas comprise the core of sustained influence. As we saw in the opening story that growing in one of these areas is not sufficient. Ongoing growth in character, competence, and commitment is required for effective, long-term influential leadership. Let's look at each of these areas carefully.

The Core of Influence
Character: The Weight of Moral Authority
Character: *The combination of moral qualities apart from intellect and talent by which a person is judged. Moral or ethical strength.*

Strong character has been generally and historically understood as essential to strong leadership. The more recent trend toward the belief that character does not matter is a failed notion that destroys many leaders. Moral choices in private as well as in public are necessary for a leader to have the empowering weight of moral authority.

Without the weight of moral authority, there is no reason for followers to believe in and trust their leader. Journalist Edward R. Murrow put it correctly and succinctly when he said: "To be persuasive we must be believable; to be believable we must be credible; to be credible, we must be truthful."[1] A leader who pays the price to practice truthfulness over time proves himself/herself to be persuasive. Stephen Covey furthers this thought when he states, "Trustworthiness is based on character, what you are as a person, and competence, what you can do. Without character and competence, we won't be considered trustworthy, nor will we show much wisdom in our choices and decisions."[2]

It is easier to agree on the necessity of character than to agree on the specific traits that make up "character." When you list specific traits, you may come to the unsettling inner awareness that you do not adequately exemplify these traits in your own life and leadership. Virtue is much easier to affirm than to live.

However, when we get specific about the character traits needed for influential leadership, our growth in these areas can begin. Until we get specific, any discussions about the necessity of character are just so many words. Influential leaders must exemplify and grow in the following traits throughout their lives:

- Endurance and hard work
- Honesty
- Loyalty
- Self-sacrifice
- Love for others
- Moral purity
- Excellence
- Serving others

You develop these traits as you learn to under-stand their meaning, value, and application in all areas of life. They become a part of you as you intentionally choose them, especially in the midst of difficult circumstances. A wise leader realizes that no matter how long she has practiced a char-acter trait, she must be vigilant to choose it again.

As your responsibilities increase and circum-stances change, aspects of your character may begin to weaken. Being loving to a newborn baby eventually becomes a part of who you are. When the child progresses into the "terrible twos," love may become a more difficult choice. In the work-place, loyalty may be an easy choice when your job is engaging and monetarily lucrative. When your job becomes stressful with fewer opportunities for bonuses, practicing loyalty usually becomes a much harder choice.

Character is displayed in speech and actions, in public and private, twenty-four hours a day. A leader is never off the clock or off the record in his display of character. The goal is not moral perfec-tion or pretense; it is rather the persistent pursuit of those attributes that will establish and build moral authority.

The ballast that truly great individuals possess is the weight of moral authority. By moral author-ity, I mean the weight and respect that belongs to those whose lives have consistently modeled rectitude, service, and humility. This ballast keeps them upright and on course, despite the challenges and opposing forces that come their way. Through the years, their lives exhibit a sense of weight and constancy that buffers them from fads and distractions. The course of their lives remains true.

Competence: The Weight of Developed Ability
Competence: *A specific range of proven skill, knowledge, or ability.*

Max De Pree, Chairman of the Board of Herman Miller Incorporated, believes that "leadership needs to be a merger of competence and moral purpose committed to the common good."[3] Competence linked to strong character is greatly needed in the rapidly changing corporate cultures of this new millennium. As Jeanie Daniel Duck suggested, "Trust in a time of change is based on predictability and capability."[4] Influential leaders win the trust of their people by displaying consistent character and steadfastly demonstrating competency in leadership decisions.

As with character, specific competence skills and practices must be identified before a leader can recognize the areas in which he needs to grow. In the book *The Leadership Challenge*, authors James Kouzes and Barry Posner identify five basic leadership competencies. They identified these five elements during interviews with thousands of corporate and organizational leaders, where the authors asked for each leader's best leadership practices. The five competencies are:

- Challenging the process
- Inspiring a shared vision
- Enabling others to act
- Modeling the way
- Encouraging the heart

I would add two additional practices to this list:

- Maintaining accountability
- Maintaining personal perspective and balance

The development of these seven skills enables leaders to gather people around a shared vision and move forward toward significant accomplishments. These competencies can provide a basis for leaders to evaluate their performances and to determine areas in which they need to develop. For those who are willing to learn, these seven skills can be a powerful boost to their understanding of leadership and their development as leaders.

Sustaining a teenager's commitment to his or her family requires these same competencies from parents. Today's teenagers are bombarded with pressure from school, sports, jobs, and friends to detach emotionally and physically from their family. Complicating this pressure is the natural transition during the teen years from familial dependence to familial independence. However, I believe, that a strong tie to family during the teen years is very important for any teen's moral and emotional development.

It takes purposeful, thoughtful, and skilled leadership on the part of the parent to challenge the process of teenage detachment from the family and to inspire a vision of the goodness that comes from remaining an integral part of the family. This vision gives the teenager compelling reasons to stay engaged in the family, it exemplifies the parent's commitment to the family and it provides opportunity for the parent to affirm the important role their child has in the family. Beyond this, parents must be vigilant in their accountability to the family and the community in which it exists, and must never lose sight of building balance and perspective in life. Without accountability, the future of the family is endangered. Without balance and perspective, the quality and benefit of the parent's leadership is compromised.

In a marriage, family, or corporation, if you want to be a leader, you have to be a learner. Learning to master these seven competencies is a lifetime project. In different circumstances and contexts and with different kinds of people, these competencies take different shapes.

As you consistently apply the seven competencies in your different leadership endeavors, skill and mastery begin to build. You must be careful to never fall into the deceitful trap of thinking yourself an expert. As Denis Waitley says so well in his book *Empires of the Mind*, "Leaders who continue learning throughout their lives never forget that they always have more to learn. The most compelling reason not to think like an expert is that your assumptions may damage your ability to generate and work with new ideas."[5] To be a leader, you must be a learner.

As I stated earlier, Rick and Cynthia each hold one piece of the three-piece leadership puzzle. Rick has character. Cynthia has competence. Both need to gain each other's strengths. Yet, even if they both possessed strong character and strong competence, neither would be a true leader without the third piece of the leadership puzzle—commitment. It is character, competence, **and** commitment together that comprise the core of sustained influence.

Commitment: The Weight of Focused Attention

Commitment: *An agreement or pledge to do or be something.*

Commitment is the clutch that engages the gears of character and competence. A leader's character and competence are inconsequential unless the leader's commitment to his or her constituents, the organization as a whole, and the organization's mission engage them. It is through commitment that the leader focuses his or her constituents' attention to the specific leadership challenges that they face together.

As the leader focuses his abilities, energy, and time, he helps to ensure success in the challenge before him and his followers. A leader who does not focus his ability, energy, and time on the leadership challenge before him becomes a saboteur of his constituents' success. His lack of commitment is an abandonment of leadership.

In this chapter's opening story, Jerry has a commitment decision to make concerning his leadership of Rick and Cynthia. He could commit to engage his character and competence in helping them develop as leaders. In so doing, there is the potential for Rick and Cynthia to become better leaders; and for their teams, to become positive and productive forces in the corporation. Jerry could also choose to do nothing. If he chooses to abdicate his responsibility to foster their development, he will watch them continue their inadequate approaches to leadership and will eventually have to fire them. Jerry can either engage or abandon.

Marriage and parenting require the same commitment. It is tough to remain focused on leading your family, especially when you have the same choices as Jerry. You can either engage your character and competence by committing your time, energy, and abilities to your family—or not. Choosing not to pour all of your character and leadership competencies into your family is abandonment, which is one of the cruelest forms of relational injury. The long-term effects on other members of the family can last for a lifetime.

However, there are times when a leader should not commit herself to a specific project or task. Wise leaders realize that they must commit to leading in only a few areas at a time in order to focus their attention. A leader must establish priorities and strategies that she believes will ensure the overall success of the team. A good leader should choose not to commit to a specific task or goal that she does not believe is the best for all involved. A good leader cannot, however, walk away from her team and abandon her leadership of it.

Three Aspects of Commitment

There are three aspects of the leader's commitment that need to be examined carefully: defining, communicating, and living your commitment.

1. Defining Your Commitment. From the outset, a leader must define his commitment as clearly and concisely as possible. This discipline will force him to think clearly about what the endeavor is going to require of him and how he will pay this price. Leaders who do not think through the costs before making commitments are setting themselves up for added stress and potential failure. Influential leaders realize that with each commitment, they place their integrity on the line. Because of this, they count the costs **before** they commit.

Defining your commitment involves thinking through the following areas:
- The role you will play (and the roles you will not play)
- The boundaries you will live by
- How you will balance what is good for the individual with what is good for the organization
- The values by which you will operate

A leader who does not define these areas will have them defined for her by her constituents' expectations and by the crises that inevitably develop. Leaders recognize there will be "crunch times" in every project that require additional commitment. By defining their commitments, leaders keep "crunch times" the exception and not the rule.

2. Communicating Your Commitment. If a leader does not communicate his commitment, he encourages his constituents to speculate and develop unfounded expectations. When a leader explains what to expect from him, he allays unfounded expectations and secures the commitment he is making.

Consider the following when you express your commitment:

- Realize you are putting your integrity on the line
- Communicate clearly, concisely, and early
- State your commitment verbally and, if appropriate, in writing

People will expect you to do what you promise, so phrase your commitments carefully. If you tell your team that they can call you twenty-four hours a day, you should be cordial when they call at 3:00 a.m. If you tell your children that you will coach their soccer team and attend every game, you should fulfill that commitment to the letter. When you commit, you draw a line in the sand of integrity. As a lifestyle leader, your life must back up your commitments.

3. Living Out Your Commitment. A leader fulfills her commitments in the same way that she proves her character: in speech and actions, in public and private, twenty-four hours a day. This reality should inspire leaders to make commitments carefully. Each new commitment impinges upon every other commitment already made. Each new commitment is also another line drawn in the sand of integrity. You must choose well when you commit.

Media events and photo opportunities are often mistaken as indicators of a leader's commitment. The CEO who shows up with the staff photographer for fifteen minutes at a company party is posturing, not leading. The father who smiles broadly in the family portrait may or may not be fulfilling his commitment to his wife and children. The proof of commitment is rarely evident when the camera is filming. Commitment is proven daily, as a leader engages his abilities, energies, and time with his commitments.

Leadership as a lifestyle flows from your character, competence, and commitment. All three elements are necessary for true leadership, and all three must be engaged fully. As you engage these three core elements, they give you the weight of influence you need to lead people to pursue high values and high performance.

The Foundations of Long-Term Leadership

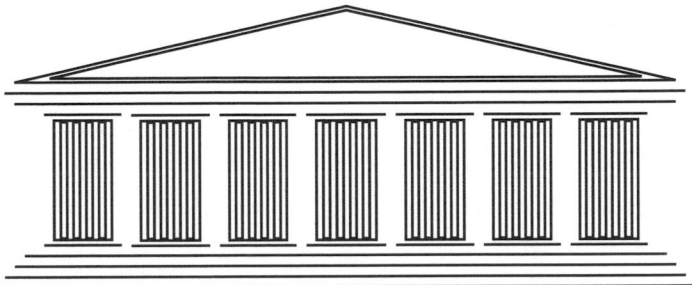

COMPETENCE
Effective pursuit
of the seven tasks
of a leader

CHARACTER
Moral and ethical
qualities and
strength

COMMITMENT
To the task, people,
organization, and
long-term values

4 · Influence with Integrity

Alignment with Core Beliefs and Virtues

Chameleons are a wonder to watch, but an exasperation to follow.

Jim was learning a difficult leadership lesson at a time of midlife evaluation. Interestingly enough, this realization came as a result of having dinner with his wife, Helen, his Vice President of Sales, Rob Chittington, and Rob's wife, Sarah.

Dinner had been a celebration of the two couples' twentieth anniversaries. Four years ago, Jim finally convinced Rob to come work for his company, and since then Rob had been a great addition to the organization. He had also been a great sounding board and friendly critic for Jim. Expanding the company had been much more difficult for Jim than he could have ever imagined.

Rob's trusted input and proven expertise were valuable assets to the company and to their friendship.

As the friends lingered over dessert and coffee, Helen posed a revealing question to Rob. "In the four years that you have worked with Jim," Helen asked, "what have you learned about him that you didn't know before." A quick smile brightened Rob's face as he considered the question. Rob loved to receive feedback and likewise enjoyed opportunities to give feedback. Jim braced himself, realizing that his true friend would be candid.

With sincerity, Rob quickly mentioned a number of Jim's strengths, giving examples of each. He then turned to a specific challenge that he believed was before Jim. "Jim," Rob thoughtfully continued, "I believe that your leadership is hampered by your desire for security and significance. Personally, I know you as a man of great integrity. But in your leadership at work, you are often like a chameleon, constantly changing in order to avoid risks and win praise. Chameleons are a wonder to watch, but an exasperation to follow."

An ancient Jewish proverb says, "Faithful are the wounds of a friend."[1] Rob was indeed a faithful friend. As the two wives stared downward, wondering how they could redirect the conversation to the happiness of the occasion, Jim responded to Rob's comments. "You've always been an honest voice of insight for me, Rob. You are, most of the time, right on the mark. Let's get together for breakfast and you can explain to me further what you see. And let's keep meeting each week until we both believe that I have begun to address the problem."

Rob happily agreed to Jim's breakfast plan and reiterated the strengths that he saw in Jim's life and leadership. The dinner ended as it had begun, with enjoyment and appreciation for the years of marriage and the years of the two couples' friendships. As Jim and Helen drove home, Helen commented on Jim's levelheaded response to Rob's comment. Jim replied, "I really believe that Rob is on to something. Too many times I feel like a chameleon, trying to figure out what color I must become next in order to play things safe and prove my worth to others. As a leader, I'm constantly shifting, not firmly planted in my convictions. I don't understand all of the reasons I act this way, but I know this isn't the leader I want to be."

Integrity: The Test of Influence

"I know that this isn't the leader that I want to be." This isn't an easy admission for anyone to make, but Jim's feeling that he isn't living up to his leadership potential is common. As the years of our lives pass and the weight of our responsibilities increase, weariness and spiritual erosion can begin to wear down the quality of our influence. Our focus as leaders can become fixed on our own basic desires such as survival, personal comfort, peace, and success. As this happens, our leadership shifts focus, realigning toward self-protection and self-serving goals, rather than centering on service to others.

This shift of leadership focus is not only a shift to selfish purposes, but also a shift away from the foundation that gives adequate boundaries and meaning to our leadership. The character, competence, and commitment of a lifestyle leader must be coherent, with a clearly defined set of beliefs and virtues. These beliefs and virtues contain what we understand about truth and the noble purposes we are called to accomplish. Leadership founded upon truth and noble purposes stays focused on service to others, rather than service to self. This type of leadership is rooted in constancy and stability, rather than the ever-shifting, chameleon-like leadership in which beliefs and virtues have been replaced with personal goals.

Jim in the opening story is a leader whose leadership has shifted. He finds himself in his early forties with a broken leadership compass. He is a good guy who wants to be a good leader, but the internal compass that guides and shapes his leadership is pointing in the wrong direction. It continuously points the direction of personal security and personal significance, rather than the direction of core beliefs and virtues. Though he realizes his compass is askew, it is hard for him to determine how he is off-track as a leader and what he must do to get back on the right path. However, what he does realize is that he continually changes according the circumstances, and that this is not the kind of leader he wants to be.

Jim's broken compass also affects his leadership in his marriage and family. It is impossible to lead well as a husband and father without being vulnerable. Marital and parental love are all about giving oneself in ways that may be rejected or ignored. In the different stages of marriage and parenting, spouses and parents need accurate compasses that constantly point toward the things that are true and noble purposes. When, like Jim, we have lost our sense of purpose and direction, self-protection and self-absorption can bring us to the abandonment of lifestyle leadership in our families. We may detach from our spouse and kids into our own little world, or we may constantly posture in order to win affection; we may also shift toward manipulation of family members to prove to others our leadership's success. Each of these shifts is selfish and proves destructive to everyone involved.

It is only when our leadership is coherent, with solid core beliefs and virtues, that we will have the moral and spiritual boundaries that we need to accomplish the noble purposes to which we are called. Core beliefs are those foundational truths that give the most accurate explanation of life and life's meaning and purpose. Virtues are those fixed and certain standards against which behavior could and should be measured. These beliefs and virtues provide that foundation to which our character, competence, and commitment must be tied. We can lead with integrity only when our character, competence, and commitment are tied to and flow from our core beliefs and virtues. To whatever degree our character, competence, and commitment are detached from our core beliefs and virtues, our leadership will be proportionately compromised.

Leadership That Reflects Integrity

CHARACTER • COMPETENCE • COMMITMENT

COHERENCE
with Core Beliefs and Virtues

Leaders who have this type of integrity are able to use their internal moral strength to positively impact the lives they influence and in the organizations they serve. Rather than fluctuating with every change, like the fickle chameleon, true leaders lead with constancy and stability. Over time their core beliefs and virtues give predictability and boundaries to their decision-making, which grants them the respect and trust of those that they lead. They are free to lead and free to serve.

It is the leader's integrity that qualifies him for influence. To be of substance and value, our influence must pass the tests of purpose, effect, trustworthiness, and lasting impact. These tests qualify or invalidate the influence that flows from our leadership. For lifestyle leaders, passing these tests is critical.

The Purpose of Influence
Our core beliefs and virtue determine the purpose of our influence. They point us to what our influence must provide to the people and the

organizations that we serve. If we have shifted away from core beliefs and virtues, the purpose of our influence may only be about manipulating others to serve our purposes. This is leadership with a broken compass. Leadership with integrity seeks to exert influence that is fixed upon the purposes of strong achievement, personal development, and service to others. We want those we lead to accomplish strong achievements that are tied to noble purposes. We also want them to develop into people who live according to core beliefs and virtues. Finally, we want to prove ourselves to be servant leaders who help others commit to a life of service as well.

The Effect of Influence

As quoted earlier in this book, lifestyle leaders believe their lips should persuade and their lives command. Those who lead with integrity develop the kind of lives that have command. With the above-mentioned purposes in mind, their lives provide their constituents with a model and guide for strong achievement, personal development, and service to others. It is the constituent's decision to align himself with these purposes. It is the lifestyle leader's responsibility to exert the kind of personal influence and integrity that convinces the constituent of the value of these purposes.

The Trustworthiness of Influence

The process of influence is a two-way street. When being led, we should first always ask the questions of trust: *Is this person trustworthy? In following this person, will I grow in becoming the person that I want to be and in accomplishing those things that are important? Is this person really committed to my benefit? Does this person know what he is talking about? How have others benefited from following this person?* These are among the questions of trust that we must ask and answer as we follow and are influenced by others. Leaders with broken compasses prove to be conflicted as they undergo the test of trustworthiness. It is hard for them to commit to people and processes that are not focused on their own needs. Leaders with integrity provide daily proof of their commitment to strong achievement, the development of others, and service to others. Their lives are their final answers to the questions of trust.

The Lasting Impact of Influence

The final test of influence is the test of its longevity and lasting impact. A leader who is aligned with timeless beliefs and virtues will tend to impact others in ways that have a positive lifelong effect. This kind of leader is not about dispensing fads, puffery, and superficialities. This leader is rather living in a way that is coherent with his or her core beliefs and virtues. Through their leadership, these leaders teach others how to live. These lessons are of great value for the entirety of their constituents' lives, not just for the time that they serve with their leader. As a result of their integrity, the influence of the lifestyle leader comes with a "lifetime guarantee."

The Danger of Squishy Values

Some may find it strange or antiquated that I speak of alignment with core beliefs and virtues rather than core beliefs and values. We live in an age where there is seemingly endless attention given to values and only suspicion or ridicule given to the older concept of virtues. It is my belief that the growing interest in values and leadership only makes us more cynical and less trusting of our leaders.

At the foundation, the cynicism that many feel for our contemporary leaders is a result of the erosion of the meaning of values in our country. Simply put, in our country, values are not near what they used to be. At the time of the founding of our nation, values were based upon universal, moral absolutes. But since then, they have gradually lost this foundation. This understanding of values being based in moral absolutes is clearly seen in the Declaration of Independence where it is stated, "We hold these truths to be self-evident, that all men are created equal, that they are endowed by their Creator with certain unalienable rights, that among these are life, liberty and the pursuit of happiness." These rights which we regard as part of our country's greatest values were understood by those who launched our country as coming from their Creator to whom they were accountable. Values have degenerated in our time to become no more than individualized preferences that are determined by circumstance and context.

Noted historian Gertrude Himmelfarb's book, *The Demoralization of Society*, puts forward the argument that there is a categorical difference between the concepts of values and virtues. She argues that values are based upon the "assumptions that all moral ideas are subjective and relative, that they are mere customs and conventions, that they have a purely instrumental, utilitarian purpose, and that they are peculiar to specific individuals and societies."[2] Ms. Himmelfarb also contends that the concept of virtues of the late eighteenth and early nineteenth centuries meant "fixed and certain standards against which behavior could and should be measured... And when conduct fell short of those standards, it was judged in moral terms, as bad, wrong or evil— not, as is more often the case today, as misguided, undesirable or 'inappropriate'."[3]

When values have been separated from a foundation of morality, they come to mean nothing because they mean anything, or even everything. In a culture where all values are deemed equal, the notion of being a values-driven leader means very little. The cynical attitude toward principled leaders today is a result of the diminished meaning and authority that today's values have in our lives and in our choices.

Leadership in a society that has separated values from morality requires clear and reflective thinking. Before individuals put themselves forward as ethical leaders, they would do well to determine their basic understanding of ethics and morality. Does the leader understand her behavior as being molded by standards of virtue and thereby evaluated by these standards? Are her life and leadership based upon moral absolutes or upon cultural and managerial expediencies?

Living with alignment to a clear set of virtues sustains a leader's influence. Living aligned to a squishy set of values leaves the leader with a finger in the air, trying to determine the direction of the wind. Lifestyle leaders realize that for their influence to remain strong, it must be based upon a strong foundation. The pull toward compromise is powerful in its effect on the leader's character, competence, and commitment.

Integrity: Choosing Against Compromise

Leaders who shift from a basis of core beliefs and virtues run the great danger of compromising the character, competence, and commitment that is at the core of their influence. When alignment with these beliefs and virtues is weakened or broken, the leader begins to make the following compromises.

Compromised Character—Devaluing the People

Without the guidance and constraint of beliefs and virtues, the leader's character begins to shift toward posturing for the sake of expediency. Rather than living in a way that establishes moral authority, the leader begins to be self-protective and self-motivated. As he shifts towards serving himself, he devalues those that he leads. Instead of constraining himself so that he can be of greater service to others, he chooses to live for himself and ignore others. His character takes on chameleon-like traits as he presents himself and interacts with others in whatever ways necessary for success.

Compromised Competence—Redefining the Mission

The seven leadership competencies mentioned in Chapter 3 require sacrifice and focus. These competencies are the kinds of things that leaders must do to positively engage others in accomplishing a worthy mission and a noble purpose. Leaders with broken compasses prove to be ineffective in leading people in any specific direction, much less toward accomplishing a worthy mission that is linked to a noble purpose. The costs involved in truly great leadership—such as vulnerability, sacrifice, humility and service—cause many leaders to abandon these seven competencies for selfish and often narcissistic reasons. They redefine the mission to protect and ensure their own personal success.

Compromised Commitment—Trivializing the People and the Mission

As stated earlier, the leader's commitment is the clutch that engages the gears of her character and competence. The leader's commitment to the people, organization, and its mission is essential. She will need the strength that comes from core beliefs and virtues to make and keep her commitments as a leader. Without beliefs and virtues, she has little basis to make and keep commitments, and will thereby waste opportunities to lead her constituents and to serve her organization. In other words, she will be drawn toward trivializing the people and the mission in order to ensure her own security and establish her significance. With a leader's undeviating commitment to the essentials, a solid foundation of core beliefs and virtues provide a basis for strong commitments. Without this foundation, commitments crumble.

Alignment: Positive Influence Tied to Ultimate Reality

We began this chapter with Jim at a midlife evaluation of his leadership. Where should he start in the journey toward becoming a lifestyle leader? More importantly, where should we start? How do we come to grasp the timeless core beliefs and virtues that will guide us as leaders, those beliefs and virtues that will provide the basis for our integrity as leaders? Those that we lead, our employees, spouses, and children, could be positively impacted for the rest of their lives if we pay the price to become leaders with integrity. But where do we begin?

What we need is bedrock. We need to drill down deep to find those truths that can sustain and guide us for a lifetime. No pop psychology or trendy philosophy will work. These faddish phenomena are shifting sand, not solid foundations.

Neither is there a need for religion that detaches us from reality. Our families, our employees, and our fellow citizens are real people who need real leadership that works in the real world. The bedrock we need must be able to engage, define, and interpret the realities of our everyday lives and leadership challenges.

Finding and aligning ourselves with this kind of bedrock is a lifelong process. It requires study, reflection, and intentional practice. It also requires that we be willing to embrace truths and practices that may be contrary to more recent cultural beliefs and moirés. Our goal should not be to become a leader that perfectly matches with today's culture; that is to become a chameleon. Our goal should be to become a leader who has integrity, whose life exemplifies constancy and stability.

Our great hope is that with our spouses, children, and employees, we will be leaders whose positive influence stands the tests of time and the rigors of life. We will lead not just to get things done, but because it is part of our calling. We lead because we want others to know the benefits of living a life that is firmly based upon truth and virtue.

For the lifestyle leader, each day is a test of alignment with core beliefs and virtues. Such questions may include:

- What are the purposes and beliefs for which I am living today?
- Is my influence today reflective of my core beliefs and virtues?

- Do I have reason to believe that those who follow my leadership are being enriched and ennobled?
- In what specific ways can I today reduce the gap between what I believe and what I live?

As we ask and answer these test questions we take seriously the reminder given to us by Jim in the opening story that we don't want to be chameleons. We don't want to be leaders who have broken or lost their compasses. We must pay the daily price of alignment. As we do this, we will need the help of God to transcend our limitations and to gain those things that we can only find in Him.

5 · The Necessity of Transcendence

Source and Foundation

Stephanie drove home with tears rolling down her cheeks. For the second quarter in a row, her sales team had not produced their numbers. Elena, Stephanie's manager, told her in no uncertain terms that if the numbers didn't significantly turn around in the third quarter, she would be replaced as team leader. As usual, Elena was fair but firm.

Although this confrontation was certainly the catalyst for the tears, something else kept them flowing as she drove the 30-minute commute home. She was running as hard as she could, striving each day to be the best that she could be. She went to seminar after seminar, read all the self-help books, and attended weekend retreats to try to improve her life. But now, she felt she couldn't sit through even one more "change your life" program—she simply couldn't face any more failure.

She had become a training junkie, but nothing she had tried had really helped her. The stark reality was that her best was not good enough. Stephanie felt defeated by life.

As she turned into the driveway, she thankfully noted that Frank was already home. He was the one constant in her life. Their love and friendship through 18 years of marriage had not been perfect, but it certainly was a place where she could relax. Even so, Stephanie had her own concerns about Frank's well being. She believed that if he honestly opened up, he would voice the same quiet desperation that she felt. They both knew that their newly elected mayor had made the performance of Frank's department a campaign issue. Being a manager in city government was often a great place to become a scapegoat.

"How was your day?" Frank asked as Stephanie entered the kitchen.

"To be honest, Frank," she replied, "I am ready to quit life."

"One request before you quit," Frank sadly smiled. "Take a look at Julie's report card. She's flunking math and has a D in English. Three of her teachers have requested conferences."

As Stephanie glanced at the report card, she felt her eyes welling up again. As she looked at Frank, she felt his frustration. He had worked so hard with Julie on math, and thought that they had made some headway. As they hugged, he surprised her by saying, "I really wonder if we're just missing something. We work as hard as we can and it seems that all we gain is more frustration and more circumstances that we can't control. We just can't make life work!"

Stephanie prepared dinner wondering what they were missing. They were two good people who lived under the weight of circumstances that they couldn't control. Sometimes she just wished she could for a moment transcend their circumstances and see what their challenges looked like from above and not just below.

Source and Foundation: Within, Around, or Beyond

The challenges of life, and especially of leadership, have the potential to crush or slowly unravel good people. It is true that one of the ways you can get through life is through unrelenting endurance. You can decide that no matter what, you'll hang in there. There are, however, some moments in life when your energy and perspective are so utterly depleted that you don't know if you can keep your head above water, and aren't really sure if you want to. "If this is what my life is going to be like," you might say to yourself, "maybe I should just quit."

For leaders, there can be the added weight of realizing that, at least during trying periods, your life is more of an unsolvable puzzle than a model for others. You might begin to seriously wonder if your best move as a leader would be to remove yourself from the leadership position. But as many people have learned, stepping down from your leadership position does not resolve the conflict that you feel within. In fact, abdicating your leadership role can actually exacerbate the feelings of helplessness.

At moments of life evaluation, we usually begin by focusing either on our circumstances or on those people around us. However, we eventually realize that we ourselves are in greatest need of change due to our blurred perspective and weariness. Questions flow through our minds: "What is it that I need to be?" "What is it I am supposed to accomplish with my life?" "Where can I gain the strength and wisdom I need to be the person and leader that I am meant to be?" We realize that we are longing to find a source that we can draw from and a foundation upon which we can build.

A Source That Gives Definition and Purpose

Two of the most basic questions in life are "Who am I to be?" and "What am I to do?" Another way of asking these questions is, "What is the definition for my life and within the scope of that definition, what am I meant to accomplish?" These questions assume several things. They assume that there is a design or purpose for our lives. They also assume that we have a responsibility for discerning that purpose and for pursuing its formation.

So where do we find the answers to these difficult questions? Do we find answers through personal introspection and reflection? To many people, turning inward appears to be a good path to take. Unfortunately, because we are not self-created, it is difficult to accept that we should be self-defined. If there is a Designer, is it not from Him that we learn the meaning and purpose of the design? Gazing within, we tend to find ideas, emotions, and dreams that may give some guidance, but that cannot be a source of definition and purpose we can pursue with certainty. An ancient Jewish proverb reminds us, "There is a way which seems right to a man, but its end is the way of death."[1] Looking inside, we gain some perspective, but we do not find a certain source for understanding who we are to be and what we are to do.

Perhaps the source is not within us but rather around us. Perhaps there is a guru, mentor, sage, counselor, or philosopher who has our answer. As Stephanie in this chapter's opening story believed, perhaps there is a seminar or retreat that can give us the answers for which our frustrations are crying out. The value of the right kind of gurus, mentors, sages, counselors, and philosophers is undeniable. As the proverb explains, "He who walks with wise men will be wise," and "With those who receive counsel is wisdom."[2] We can often gain very practical help from seasoned men and women who share their insights. Most of us rarely access this kind of life wisdom, and those that we lead suffer as a result. But are even the wisest advisors truly able to answer the questions of the meaning and purpose of our lives?

Looking for the answer to who we are to be and what we are to do in others is actually an extension of introspection. If in ourselves there are limited answers to these questions, why should we think that some other person could be the source of our answers? Experience, reflection, and introspection give limited answers to our questions of meaning and purpose, regardless of the source. As we struggle in life and leadership, we realize that we long for transcendence, not imminence, for revelation, not speculation.

Recently, at the conclusion of a leadership training program I conducted for an agency of the United States government, someone said to me, "From your presentation today, I realized that there is a spiritual dimension to leadership development." Her comment surprised me because, during the three-and-a-half-hour program, no one, including myself, had mentioned religion or spirituality. As we faced in the training some of the tough decisions and commitments that are required of lifestyle leaders, she rightly discerned that leadership ultimately brings us face-to-face with our mortal limitations and our need for a source of strength beyond ourselves. Lifestyle leadership requires clear thinking about our need for God and for substantive movement toward His transcendent perspective and guidance.

A Foundation That Gives Strength

Leadership is a process of change that takes place in changing contexts and within changing people. Leaders work with their constituents to affect change. The contexts in which they exert leadership, whether in the corporation or the family, in the United States or elsewhere, are also changing. Moreover, those that they lead are all going through the never-ending changes that life and life choices bring. Over time, the struggle to shore up our leadership efforts on the shifting sands of circumstance can exhaust even the strongest of leaders. Employees quit, corporations downsize or merge, and kids grow up and grow on. It is hard to aim for sustained influence when everything around us is in some state of flux.

With change comes uncertainty. Will you be smart enough, strong enough, and have the resources necessary to lead well as the people and organization around you change? Will you be able to have sustained impact as things change, or will you eventually be overwhelmed or left behind? Will your accomplishments as a leader eventually wash away in the ever-changing tides that swirl around you? It is tempting to wonder if your work as a leader will have any lasting impact.

Change and its uncertainties make us realize our need for a foundation upon which to build our life and leadership, a foundation that will give us reason to believe that over time, our influence will stand firm. We see this need when we realize that we are not strong enough, smart enough, in control enough, rich enough, good enough, or wise enough to affect the long-term influence that we want to have. Like Stephanie and Frank in the opening story, we cannot exert the kind of long-term, positive influence that we want in our careers or in our families on the strength of our wills alone. It is not that we are unwilling; it is that in the long term, we are unable.

Unfortunately, even a sure foundation for your leadership does not guarantee that everything will turn out the way you want. Change will continue to occur. A sure foundation will, however, help sustain your influence in the midst of change. Just as a house that is built on a solid foundation is more likely to stand firm in the midst of storms, so our life's influence needs a firm foundation in order to endure the changes and challenges that will come over time. But is there such a foundation, and where can we find it?

One night in La Jolla, California, I was speaking to the executive leaders of a healthcare products manufacturer. When I suggested to them that long-term, effective leaders needed to ask and answer the questions related to source and foundation, the president of the company stated, "So you are talking about religion." Asking his permission to speak personally, I explained briefly how my faith had been the true source and foundation of my life. The executives then broke into a very positive discussion, and the evening concluded with the president stating that it had been the best presentation on leadership that he had ever attended. Just like Frank and Stephanie, these leaders saw the need for a source and foundation.

In this postmodern era, it is out of vogue to think of a transcendent God that is beyond us and yet accessible to us. Contemporary culture and philosophy are much more supportive of a secularized redefining of faith that divorces it from a basis in a transcendent God. This redirection toward a "faith" that is individualized and internalized offers much more hope that it can actually deliver. It is the image of hope that each morning has to face the reality in the mirror.

The Secularization of Faith: The Image of Hope, the Reality in the Mirror
The Age of Personal Sovereignty

Charles Handy is a very intelligent British management writer who was educated at both Oxford and MIT. He is a former executive with Shell Oil Company and Professor at the London Business School. In 1998, he wrote a book entitled *The Hungry Spirit*, which is subtitled *Beyond Capitalism: A Quest for Purpose in the Modern World*. In the book, Handy explains his personal philosophy that he calls "Proper Selfishness." Handy's treatment of religion in his book is a great example of secularized faith.

In his chapter entitled "The Age of Personal Sovereignty," Handy includes a section on "The Religious Option." In this section, he speaks of the helpfulness of religious settings and meditation. He affirms that these can be very invigorating "Turkish baths for the soul."[3] He then gives the following conclusion:

> Religion like this is a great aid to self-responsibility. It might even be essential. But it is religion without the creeds and without the hierarchies. It is the religion of doubt and uncertainty, offer-

ing one the strength to persevere, to find one's own way in a world that is, inevitably, very different from any world that was known to those who went before.[4]

Handy's comments on religion are very revealing. When he divorces religion from creeds and relegates it to the fog of doubts and uncertainty, he simultaneously divorces it from a transcendent God who serves as a source and foundation for His creation. Handy's religion directs us to keep looking within ourselves for the answers to our questions about who we are to be and what we are to do. It is a religion more about ourselves and our hoped-for personal sovereignty.

Handy's notions on religion are very fitting with the spirit of our age. However, I believe these tenets fail to satisfy the hungry spirits of men and women like Frank and Stephanie. I believe that leadership serves a God-given purpose of bringing us to the end of our own abilities in order to see our need for an external, transcendent God.

The Created Denying Their Creator

I stated earlier that in the beginning God made man in His own image, and ever since man has been attempting to return the favor. In the western world, this desire to remake God in our image began during the Renaissance period, as exemplified by Michelangelo's statue of David, the Jewish King. Two aspects of David's body as depicted by the artist are striking: The lack of circumcision and the size of the hands.

The historical David was undoubtedly circumcised as a newborn Jewish child to indicate that he was a child of God's covenant people. God commanded this practice for all Jewish newborn boys. The statue of David communicates through its lack of circumcision that David is to be remembered for something apart from his religious faith and heritage. The hands of the statue also reveal a great deal about the artist's attitudes. Michelangelo created the statue's hands disproportionately large in comparison with the rest of his body.[5] Michelangelo's David was a statement of humanistic hope that no longer recognized the need for a transcendent God. David was not to be remembered for his faith but rather for his physical beauty and accomplishments achieved through the strength of his hands.

The David of history would have not recognized himself in this statue, not only as a result of his physical appearance, but also because of his self-confessed need for the transcendent God. He expressed his need as follows: "Find rest, O my soul, in God alone; my hope comes from him. He alone is my rock and my salvation; he is my fortress, I will not be shaken. My salvation and my honor depend on God; he is my mighty rock, my refuge."[6]

David was a brilliant military and governmental leader who clearly recognized his need for God. The statue of David would fit well with Handy's philosophy of "Proper Selfishness." David, the King of Israel, would not fit with this philosophy at all. He was a leader who throughout his failures and successes saw himself as a creature who was defined and sustained by his Creator.

The Dilemma of Attempting to Be Creator

When we look at ourselves in the mirror each morning, few of us think that we are viewing a god. Most mornings we look like scraggly creatures, not like gods who can sustain our need for a source and a foundation. It is hard to fool the person in the mirror into really believing that we can be our own god, or, as Charles Handy would say, our own sovereign.

Our dilemma lies in the fact that we in our modern times believe that we want a transcendent God who will answer our questions but not interfere with our autonomy. We want a Sovereign who isn't really sovereign. As time goes on, we begin to refashion God into a deified reflection of ourselves. God takes on our image and we take on His sovereignty. This exchange sounds great in the movies and magazines of our age, but I have to believe that the God who is there finds this attempted philosophical and theological charade interesting, to say the least. Our dilemma is that we do not have the answers to our questions about source and foundation, no matter how many bait-and-switch God games we attempt. We have the potential to be great creatures. We fail miserably when we try to become our own gods.

Our attempts at playing God will fail every time. So how is it that we come to connect with the God who is there?

Connecting with the God Who Is There
Working Back from the Creature to the Creator

We can begin the journey of coming to God by studying what we learn about Him in His creation. If He is the Designer, what clues does He give us in His design? Among the clues we find in creation are beauty, diversity, unity, and interdependence. We see in humanity clues such as morality, justice, relationships, and love. Each of these clues suggests that these are things that God values and which He more fully understands than we. Another clue that we gain from creation is that its intricacy and detail, its sheer wonder and splendor, reveal God's deep regard for His creation.

When I was a young boy, the movie *The Sound of Music* was incredibly popular. This entertaining movie about the Von Trap family of Austria played at theatres for months at a time. One Sunday, our family including my grandmother went to see the movie. As the film began with its beautiful, panoramic footage of the magnificent Austrian Alps, my grandmother leaned over to me and said, "How could anyone see this and not know that there is a God?" My Grandmother, upon looking at the splendor of creation, could only conclude that it was a clear indication of a Designer/Creator. She clearly saw His fingerprints all over creation.

It is a shame that this ability to see God's fingerprints has been dulled or given up by so many in our age. In our quest for personal sovereignty and for a philosophy that explains life apart from God, we have painted ourselves into an existential corner when we need real answers to ultimate questions about life and leadership. In reality, we all eventually come to say the same thing as Frank: "God, we can't make life work." We can't make life work because we are creatures. He can because He is God.

The Commitment to Seek and Embrace

Many people seek after God in the same way they surf the Internet; they go from one god to the next, seeking something that is entertaining, motivating, or specific to their needs or interests. They do not make commitments; if promises are made, they are only one-time commitments to gain specific products or services. There are several reasons this is a deficient way to seek after God:

1. This search focuses on our needs rather than on God's truth and purposes. Those who seek after God must come to understand their needs in the light of His truth and purposes. They find Him, and then they come to more clearly understand their own needs and desires.

2. This approach focuses on seeking rather than committing. With this attitude, we are in control of the search and we protect our autono-

my. With the God who is there, this strategy will never work. As Sovereign and Creator, He requires commitment and alignment with His truth and His character.

3. The Internet surfing approach to finding God is also misguided because it does not reflect our need for help in coming to God. Those who come to God must come with humble requests for His mercy and grace.

4. Finally, this approach is deficient because it doesn't reflect the broken relationship and the wrong choices that we have made in the past. Mankind searches for Him because we have each in our own way rebelled against His sovereignty. To come to know God, we must first find His forgiveness so that the possibility of a relationship may be restored.

Connecting with the God who is there requires a commitment to seek and then to embrace Him, regardless of the cost. We do not come to God as equals or as partners wanting to cut a deal. We come as men and women who in our lives and leadership have come to the end of ourselves, or realizing that we will eventually come to the end of ourselves. We come because we need help. We are cheered by the words of the ancient Jewish prophet who served as God's voice saying: "'You will seek me and find me when you seek me with all your heart. I will be found by you,'" declares the LORD..."[7]

A Guided Journey, a Lifelong Adventure

A life of faith in the God who is there is a guided journey that encompasses all of life and death. The character and truth of God guides us daily. God's character and truth are revealed to us through His creation, His scriptures, and in His Son Jesus Christ. As we, by His grace, align ourselves with His character and truth, we come to understand how He is the source from which we learn our meaning and purpose. We also learn how His truth serves as a foundation upon which we can build our lives and leadership—and have reason to believe that over time, they will stand firm. All the days of our lives and even in our death, He will be our faithful guide to whom we must give our allegiance.

As we follow Him, we also come to find that we have embarked on a lifelong adventure in which we are continually brought to the end of ourselves in order to deepen our trust and dependence in Him. This is an adventure that requires our total engagement. His ways are not always our ways. His thoughts are not always our thoughts. By His grace we have signed on with the God who will lead us into the great adventure of learning His will and His ways. Our adventure in knowing God becomes the focal point of our lives, from which we understand how to live and lead in all of the other areas of our lives.

Every lifestyle leader will eventually say as Frank did earlier in this chapter, "God, I can't make life work." This cry for needed transcendence can be the first step to coming to know the God who can make life work, as He becomes our source and foundation. In the following chapters we will see what lifestyle leadership looks like in marriages, families, careers, friendships and heritage. It is assumed in these chapters that our relationship with God is the source and foundation from which we begin to understand how to lead in each of these spheres of influence.

For some, this assumption may not yet be reality. The following suggestions and questions will guide you as you consider your need of a transcendent source and foundation.

1. Identify the ways in which you, like Stephanie and Frank, can't make life work.

2. In what ways does your inability to make life work indicate that you have an unclear or inadequate understanding of your life's definition and purpose? How is your current source insufficient for your current challenges?

3. In what ways does your inability to make life work indicate that you have insufficient strength for sustained influence? How is your current foundation unstable or inadequate for your current challenges?

4. Are there ways in which you are trying to be your own god, your own sovereign? What linkage is there between your quest for personal sovereignty and your inability to make life work?

5. What is the basis for your current understanding of God and His purpose for your

life? In what ways do you need to seek anew the God who is there?

6. Who do you know that seems to have found God to be their Source and Foundation? What do you need to learn from them?

Questions such as these help us to move from the limits of our humanity to the fullness of God's sovereignty. Our need for a transcendent source and foundation is fully found as we seek and embrace Him.

6 · Adversity: The Path to Intimacy

Walking Through Life Together

Miles from the city, Leon pulled his car over to the side of the road at one of his favorite places. The panoramic view of the ocean reflected a magnificent yellowish orange moon light on the waters. As he looked over the ocean, his mind went back to that night six years ago when he had stopped at the same place to consider how to talk to Sheila.

On that horrible night years before, the striking beauty and majesty of the scene had drawn Leon out of his problems for an all-too brief moment. But just like the ebb and flow of the tide, Leon had been drawn back into the vastness of his challenges. He had to tell Sheila that their life was about to change, and he simply didn't know how to find the words.

Leon knew his company was going under, and the time had come to admit that there wasn't one thing left he could do to prevent it. The previous years had been the toughest period of his life, but he had always believed that he would be able to pull the company out of its nosedive and restore its profitability. He had firmly believed that he could fix the company's problems, but his confidence paled next to his wife's belief. Sheila had believed in him more than he had believed in himself. She was absolutely committed to him. Unfortunately, he had responded to her commitment by withholding from her the whole truth about the company's status. He only told her the few things that appeared to be going right, and hardly ever mentioned the great number of things that were going wrong. He needed her support, and never wanted her to see him fail. When he did mention negative developments, he always blamed them on someone else's performance, not his own.

As Leon stared out to the horizon that fateful night, he knew it was time to face facts. Sheila had no idea that the company was even close to bankruptcy. Moreover, she had no idea that Leon had personally signed on loans for the company for which they would be personally responsible. How could he tell her the truth after so many lies?

Suicide and running away were not options that he would consider. He had to tell Sheila the truth. It was the only right thing to do, and there was no way to keep the truth from her any longer. He feared that once she realized the extent of his failures she would either quietly take the kids and leave him, or stay for the sake of their family but never believe in him again. He had bro-

ken her trust and had jeopardized their financial security. The thought of telling her these things almost made him nauseous. As he looked out over the water, his failure seemed as deep and as turbulent as the ocean. As a husband, he felt that he was drowning.

That night six years ago had indeed been one of the worst nights of his life. Later that evening, when he finally told Sheila the truth, she seemed cold and paralyzed. As she looked at him, her eyes contained every hurtful emotion. She was devastated, angry and wanted to be left alone. She left the room with tears rolling down her face.

But now, six years after that confrontation, things were completely different. Leon's company did go under, its few assets liquidated, and Leon and Sheila lost their house. Their marriage was shaken to its core, but did not collapse. Sheila forgave Leon and they committed to work through their troubles together. Leon was hired as the Vice President of Human Resources for a company at which one of his friends was President. Leon slowly regained Sheila's trust and they gradually made headway financially. They had struggled together, and rebuilt their lives together.

Tonight they were eating dinner with an engaged couple from their church that had asked them to talk about how to build a good marriage. As he took one last look at the ocean before he headed off to pick up Sheila for dinner, Leon said to himself, "I sure know a lot more to say to the couple tonight than I did six years ago."

For Better or Worse...Till Death Do Us Part
Adversity Within, Adversity Without

Of all the many adjectives used to describe Hollywood, the one that most readily comes to my mind is unreal. Life as portrayed in most movies is detached from the worlds in which most, if not all, of us live. The few movies that I have seen recently don't remind me of anyone I have ever known. The characters and the way that they deal with their problems are largely foreign to the people around me and the way they face their challenges. This is certainly true of Hollywood's depictions of marriage.

In a Hollywood marriage, a couple meets, may or may not live together to try things out, gets married, and goes on their honeymoon. The honeymoon is the highpoint of the marriage. From there, the couple either abuses one another and then divorces, or lives together in a world where wrong choices don't have consequences. I cannot remember the last time that I watched a movie where the marriage portrayed reminded me of any couple I actually know.

A reality of marriage today—a reality of marriage throughout history—is that it is filled with and surrounded by adversity. Every marriage, including every great marriage, regularly involves tension, stress, frustration, and offense as the husband and wife struggle to fulfill their commitment to love each other. The calamity described in the opening story in Leon and Sheila's marriage is not atypical. Crises like these happen in marriages.

What is uncommon is the way in which Leon and Sheila dealt with the situation.

In the March 1997 issue of the *Social Forces Journal*, a study was released that compared data from young married couples of equal age in 1980 and 1992. The authors found that the 1992 couples "interacted significantly less, ate fewer meals together and went out together less often. They also fought more and had more marital problems."[1] It appears the challenges faced by today's married couples draw them away from each other. Couples find adverse circumstances within and around their marriages and allow these forces to break them apart, rather than using troubled times as a reason to pull together.

I believe that adversity is the path to intimacy in a marriage. As couples face the challenges within and around their marriages, they must commit to walk through adversity together, no matter how painful it may be. If they do this, then over the years the depth of intimacy between them will grow and flourish. They will look at each other and realize that it is with their spouse that they have faced and walked through the great challenges of life. Their intimacy grows not as a result of their life and marriage being "picture perfect." Intimacy grows because they have lived out their vows to each other and gone through life together. It is the adventure of walking through adversity together that welds a couple's hearts and wills together.

Two Humans Confronting the Undesirable

One way to define marriage is as two humans confronting the undesirable parts of themselves, their spouses, and their world. Marriage at times serves as a magnifying glass that brings out with great clarity our own weaknesses, our spouse's weaknesses, and those things that are wrong around us. The love expressed during dating, the wedding, and the honeymoon can quickly be overwhelmed by personal differences and life's disappointments.

In his book *The Marriage Builder*, Dr. Larry Crabb describes engagement in the following way. He says that the guy looks at his girlfriend and thinks that if he can marry her, he will have it all. She is beautiful, she thinks he is cute, is liked by his friends, and likes being with him. The girl looks at the guy and thinks that if she can marry him, she will be absolutely fulfilled. He is handsome, he loves being with her, is liked by her friends, and seems very ambitious. Crabb explains these attitudes with a very powerful analogy, comparing them to ticks that see the other as a great big juicy dog that they can attach to and have their needs met by. Unfortunately, when this couple marries, they wake up one day and realize that they are only two ticks with no dog.[2] Their expectations of having all of their needs met are not being fulfilled as they had hoped.

For marriages to last until "death us do part," we have to commit to confronting the undesirable parts of our marriage and ourselves. We have to agree to change what can be changed and accept what can't be changed. Marriage is not a perfect union; it is in fact a union of two imperfect people. For marriage to work we have to choose to love in spite of our weaknesses, failures, and flaws.

Divide and Conquer Becomes Divide and Divorce

One of the subtle traps that destroys marriages is the prolonged pursuit of "divide and conquer." As the stress of marriage, family, and career builds, couples can decide to forego their relationship with each other in order to cover all of their other responsibilities. They choose to divide their responsibilities, neglecting each other to conquer the challenges ahead of them. They may work different hours from each other so that someone is always home with the kids. One spouse may take a one-year international assignment that pays well so that the other spouse will not have to work and can be at home with the kids. "Divide and conquer" looks great on paper, but in life it is often disastrous.

Part of the purpose of marriage is intimacy. Sexual intimacy is only part of the intimacy that should exist in a marriage. When we choose, for whatever reason, to give up the intimate partnership of our spouse for a prolonged time, our need for intimacy does not go away. It remains, and as this need is unmet, it grows. This longing can lead to underlying anger toward our spouse that is hard to understand. It can also lead to co-dependent friendships with others or to cyber-intimacy on the Internet. Ultimately, it can lead to an adulterous relationship or to the complete loss of love for our spouse. The problem with "divide and conquer" is that, over time, the divide can become permanent.

Marriages that grow in intimacy and commitment are those relationships that keep ever before them the fact that they have made a vow to each other before God—a vow that they will choose to love each other until death parts them. As spouses, we can influence each other to "bow to our vows" by modeling the way for each other.

Influence that Bows to the Vows

Modeling the way is a leadership competency that needs exertion by both husband and wife. Each person needs to exemplify commitments that reflect a deep loyalty to each other and to the vows that they made. These commitments include the following four concepts:
- Committing to whatever it takes, for as long as it takes
- Being a door opener, not a doormat
- Being strong in conviction, but with a humble heart
- Being a catalyst of fulfillment

Whatever It Takes and As Long As It Takes

When both husband and wife determine that divorce is not an option, a world of potential opens up for a couple. Committing to do whatever it takes to live out their vows to each other provides an atmosphere in which marriage can blossom and develop, even through the hard times. In the opening story, Sheila's commitment to fulfill her vows to her husband—to do whatever it took, as long as it took—provided the context in which her husband could find forgiveness and the motivation to rebuild his leadership and trustworthiness. As is true with all human commitments of love, the commitment to fulfill our vows requires vulnerability. As we will see later, marriage isn't marriage without vulnerability.

Door Openers, Not Doormats

Couples can also model the way for each other to fulfill their vows by being door openers, not doormats. As we open doors by showing deference to each other, we communicate that we want to put the interests of our spouse before our own. Similarly, as we open doors of opportunity for each other to pursue goals or interests, we communicate that we want the best for our spouse, even if it means that we limit the pursuit of our own goals or interests.

Opening doors communicates love and respect. Becoming our spouse's doormat communicates a misguided love characterized by disrespect. In marriage, we should expect each other's respect and confront each other when disrespect occurs. Fulfilling our vows has nothing to do with condoning abuse. It has everything to do with modeling the way in deferring to each other.

Strength of Conviction, Humility of Heart

The husband and wife should live out their personal convictions in a way that encourages each other to be strong when tempted to be weak. As they each work toward daily alignment with their core beliefs and virtues, they gain the strength and perspective necessary to fulfill their vows to one another. They also remind each other of the blessing to others that comes from being a person of strong conviction.

Husbands and wives should also work toward being humble in heart. Arrogance neutralizes the influence of a person of conviction. Our aim should be to stand firm and humbly recognize the many times that we have compromised the convictions that we hold. This attitude allows us to encourage our spouses when they violate those beliefs and virtues that they know to be true. Humility builds a relationship where truth is respected and where grace is given.

A Catalyst for Fulfillment

You are responsible for your own personal fulfillment. I believe that true fulfillment is a choice and a matter of perspective that is ultimately linked to our relationship with God. Just like happiness, fulfillment is a choice. Having said this, I do believe that we should do all that we can to provide experiences that fulfill our spouse's hopes and aspirations. You can be a catalyst for your spouse's fulfillment:

- By understanding what your spouse believes God has called him or her to be and to do
- By helping your spouse become the person he or she is called to be, and by helping your spouse accomplish the goals he or she feels called to realize. Spouses grounded in the leadership proposed in this book will do all that they can to help their spouses fulfill the God-given purposes before them

These four commitments are practical ways to fulfill your vows to your spouse. In so doing, you also positively remind each other of the kind of commitment necessary for a great marriage.

"The Music Is Playing, But Only One of Us Is Dancing"

I once had a customer who was very committed to her marriage and family. However, her husband was only committed to himself and to his career. As the years went on, she sadly came to realize that she was the only one of the two who was really dedicated to the marriage and family. As she explained it to me one day, "I woke up and realized that the music is playing, but only one of us is dancing." It was a heartbreaking realization for her.

I believe that there are five decisions that keep disengagement from happening in a marriage. These five concepts are certainly not exhaustive, but serve as a great checklist to help ensure continued engagement with each other:

- Vulnerability
- Forgiveness
- Boundaries
- Love and grace
- Source and foundation

Vulnerability: It Wouldn't Be Marriage Without It

I believe growing marriages require vulnerability. As the years go on in a marriage, some couples begin to look like two turtles constantly withdrawn into their shells. This sort of relationship may be cohabitation, but it is not marriage. We cannot truly love if we don't also risk being hurt. In any marriage, given enough time, both partners will be hurt. Hurtful behavior must be confronted, but—except in extreme situations—vulnerability cannot be withdrawn. Vulnerability is a daily decision to believe the best about each other and to trust each other. It wouldn't be marriage without it.

Forgiveness: Marriage Won't Last Without It

As married people move together through the years, the offenses begin to accrue. Some hurts are comprised of common insensitivities or thoughtlessness. Others are more serious in nature. No matter the degree of the offence, all must be forgiven. Forgiveness releases us from the bondage of hurt and blame and allows us, over time, to reengage with our spouse. Forgiveness also graciously gives our spouse the privilege of starting over again. In the opening story, Sheila was willing to forgive Leon. This released her from the bitterness that naturally manifests when we have been hurt. It also graciously gave Leon the gift of a new beginning.

The foundation of our forgiveness is not our own greathearted natures. The foundation of forgiveness must be God's forgiveness of our own failures. In other words, we must forgive others just as we ourselves have been forgiven by God. Spouses that freely forgive build marriages that foster growth and acceptance. Spouses unwilling to forgive are also unwilling to give each other the gift of a new beginning. Instead, unforgiving spouses build each other boxes for which there is no escape. For spouses to stay engaged in their marriages, forgiveness must be granted. Marriage won't last without it.

Boundaries: Marriage Unravels Without Them

It is important for couples to set boundaries for which they will fulfill their vows. Boundaries are agreed upon limits that will not be violated. They provide a basis for trusting each other's judgments when discussion is not possible. Boundaries include areas such as how money will be spent, acceptable relationships with members of the opposite sex, and how much time will be spent at work. When boundaries are freely discussed and agreed upon, trust between spouses has a stronger foundation.

Couples who have not agreed upon boundaries tend to believe the worst about each other, second guess each other's decisions, and experience regular disappointments and "surprises." In the opening story, Leon realized that he had crossed the boundary of honesty by keeping information away from his wife. He had been more focused on shaping the truth than telling the truth. A boundary had been violated, and his wife and their marriage suffered because of it. Deciding to set boundaries is a decision that allows for greater trust. Over time, marriages unravel without boundaries.

Love and Grace: Marriage Burns Up Without Them

All marriages experience great amounts of friction. The friction comes from two imperfect people merging their lives together. It also comes from all of the external people and processes that impinge upon the marriage. Just as most machines need some kind of lubricant to minimize friction and its destructive effect, so marriages need a lubricant as well. I believe that love and grace are the soothing elements that both husband and wife must apply to their marriage. Choosing to love and give grace will minimize the friction between the couple and its potential destructive effect.

In the Christian faith, love is defined in the following way:

> Love is patient, love is kind. It does not envy, it does not boast, it is not proud. It is not rude, it is not self-seeking, it is not easily angered, it keeps no record of wrongs. Love does not delight in evil

but rejoices with the truth. It always protects, always trusts, always hopes, always perseveres. Love never fails.[3]

Grace is understood to be unmerited kindness, favor, and help. Both love and grace are given unconditionally, not because they are deserved. In a marriage, spouses must choose to give what is not deserved and what has not been earned. Love and grace absorb the heat of friction, helping couples move past minor offenses and focus on serious issues. Love and grace don't hide offenses, but rather remove some of the destructive heat and wear that offenses bring to bear upon a marriage. Similar to forgiveness mentioned above, the basis for giving love and grace is that you have received it from God. Love and grace are a great lubricant. Marriages burn up without them.

Source and Foundation: Marriage Is Consumed Without Them

Earlier in this book, we looked at the questions of source and foundation. Source has to do with finding the answer to your questions about who you are to be and what you are to do. Foundation has to do with finding a basis to build your life and leadership upon that will stand firm over time. I believe that spouses who have not answered these questions can bring a lot of unneeded baggage into a marriage. These unanswered questions tend to negatively impact marriage in one of two ways.

People who have not come to a clear understanding of their source and foundation begin to pressure their spouses to either become their source and foundation, or to become a guru who will lead them to the answers that they are seeking. As a friend of mine puts it, they are walking around looking for someone into which they can plug their umbilical cord. Husbands and wives cannot be their spouse's sure source and foundation. It is right for us to encourage and support each other in coming to understand who we are to be and what we are to do. But at best, we will only be able to provide limited answers to our spouses.

Unbalanced and constantly redirected lives strain the marriage's foundation. Many are continually in search of the next job, conference, experience, or relationship that will give them the answers for which they are searching. Their spouses are drawn into this world of indecision and fruitless searching. Spouses who are still wrestling with the issues of source and foundation can bring great disruption and unpredictability to a marriage. This eventually erodes the relationship.

As we come to understand in general terms what God wants us to be and to do, we can build lives and marriages that have constancy and stability. Though disruptions from without and within will occur, they can be absorbed by the strength that comes from two people who are clear about who they are to be and what they are to do. Without a clear sense of source and foundation, marriages can be consumed as spouses desperately attempt to answer these questions in misguided and ineffective ways.

The Courage to Go First

Lifestyle leaders realize that to exert the required influence, they must set the pace by going first. In other words, lifestyle leaders recognize their responsibility to model the way for others. They are willing to vulnerably and sometimes awkwardly take the first steps in accomplishing the mission and vision in a way that is aligned with agreed-upon values. Willingness to go first is the kind of lifestyle leadership needed in both husbands and wives in fulfilling their vows and making their marriages a success. The following reasons for going first can serve as reminders for husband and wife lifestyle leaders.

Because It Sets the Pace

Over the years, marriages can devolve into small-hearted exchanges of duty and responsibility. The husband takes out the trash and the wife does the laundry, but their hearts are far apart. Lifestyle leaders realize that by going first with large-hearted actions reflective of their vows, they help set the pace of generous, loving actions in a marriage. Their willingness to go first in love and sacrifice often motivates their spouse to respond in similar fashion. Going first establishes a great environment in which a marriage can grow.

Because It Proves Your Love

Don't tell your spouse you love them if you are not willing to go first in living out your vows. When actions don't follow words, your spouse will eventually understand that your words mean very little. Love is proven by actions, not by the gush of emotions or the surge of hormones. Lifestyle leaders realize that in marriage, as well as in other arenas of leadership, talk is cheap. You prove your love by going first.

Because You Made a Vow

Lifestyle leaders go first in fulfilling their vows because it is the right thing to do. Their vows were not made with built-in conditions and exception clauses. When they promised to love and cherish each other, they made a 24/7 commitment for the rest of their lives. Lifestyle leaders go first in fulfilling their vows because they promised that before God.

The reference point for trust in a marriage is the vow you make in God's presence to your spouse. It is by faithfully aligning your life with that vow, depending upon God's grace for strength and perspective, that you ultimately prove your trustworthiness to your spouse. We go first in fulfilling our vows because we want our spouse, our children, our community, and our God to know that each day we are working toward faithfulness in the most primary of human relationships. It is that important. We must go first.

The story of Leon and Sheila illustrates how intimacy grows in marriage. Committed love empowered by God turns any adversity into a great adventure toward intimacy. As a lifestyle leader in your marriage, don't take your cues from Hollywood. Take them from your vows.

7 · Family: The Seedbed for Leadership

Developing Future Leaders at Home

As first-term U.S. Congressman Chip Steiger slipped into his airplane seat, he breathed a sigh of relief. His term was over, and he would not be returning to Washington for a second term. He had run in his first election because he believed he could make a difference for the people and his country by serving in the Congress. He lost his second election because he no longer really believed that he could make a difference. His heart was no longer in the work, and the folks back home could tell. He would be glad to be back home.

He had looked forward all week to the two-hour flight home. It would be his first opportunity to think through what had happened to the optimism he had when he first went to Washington. He hadn't been naïve enough to think that Congress was going to be an easy place to exert influence, especially as a first-term Congressman.

But he quickly lost hope that he would be able to make any lasting difference at all. He came to believe that Congress simply wasn't focused on serving the people. Instead, Congress's focus was significantly diffused due to partisan politics, the incessant need for political fundraising, and the constant dilemma of dealing with the needs of opposing special interest groups. Chip had thought that the government was of the people and by the people, as the founding fathers had prescribed. But after his difficult tenure, Chip wasn't certain that government was for the people.

Chip knew that the root of his loss of optimism went deeper than his growing cynicism with Congress's focus and effectiveness. On his desk in the Congressional Office Building he had front and center a picture of his wife Claire and their sons Seth, who was 14, and Kent, just 11. Many times while working at his desk he would look at their picture and feel a knot in his gut. Day after day, as he looked at his family and felt the knot grow, he tried to figure out what he was feeling. One day, it became clear: "I don't know how to change the gridlock of Washington," he said to himself. "But I do know how to father these boys. What am I doing in Washington?" That was it! That, however, was what had given him the knot in his gut when he looked at their picture. What was he doing in Washington?

As the flight attendant refilled his coffee cup, Chip's mind was already rehearsing all of the reasons why public service was important. He couldn't deny the validity of any of the reasons. His problem wasn't with the importance of public service. His problem was determining the most important place to use his gifts and abilities. No doubt others had been more effective in their first terms than he. Chip was also confident that if he had served several more terms he would have grown in his effectiveness. But at the end of two more terms, Seth would be 18 and on his way to college and Kent would be 15, with only 3 years at home before college began.

Chip was smart enough to realize that returning home and reentering the family business could be just as time-consuming as his job in Congress. He would have to refocus his energy toward Claire and the boys, which at times would be very tough. Chip was definitely ambitious in his work. Perhaps in the future he would have more insight and a greater aptitude for refocusing the government in its service to the people. For now, he believed he needed to learn how to refocus himself as the father for his boys. "Who knows," Chip wondered, as he tasted his last sip of coffee. "Maybe I can help one of my sons lead in refocusing Washington."

The Moral Confusion of Our Future Leaders

Some realities give us dramatic reasons to be concerned about our country's future. One of these realities was revealed in a 1998 Josephson Institute for Ethics study on the ethical behavior of American teenagers. This study was a nationwide poll of 20,000 middle school and high school students. The poll had a margin of error of three percentage points.

According to the poll, "47 percent of high school students admit to stealing from a store in the past year; 70 percent admit to cheating on an exam; 92

percent confess to lying to parents."[1] Remarkably enough, 97 percent of middle school and high school students affirmed that they believed it is important for people to have good character.[2] What a confused group of students!

J. Angelo Corlett, founding editor-in-chief of the *Journal of Ethics*, made the following comment on these results: "It should sound an alarm that people don't take ethics seriously in our society, and that's been the case for some time."[3] Upon reflecting on these results, one wonders how these students understand the concept of character. Regretfully, all we have to do to better understand how they interpret character is to remember the national role models they watched as they grew up.

The Moral Confusion of Our Current Leaders

Our children's confusion regarding ethics and character is merely a reflection of what we have mirrored to them. The moral confusion of former President Bill Clinton and former Speaker of the House Newt Gingrich is sufficient enough explanation as to why our children are confused about ethics and character. Our political leaders campaigned on the promise of building the most ethical administration in our country's history, only to be elected and then further confuse our children as to what morality really means. Many of our leaders in the entertainment industry sniff at the notion of making films that have a strong ethical message linked to moral absolutes, as though such a movie were somehow intolerant or subversive. Many of our business leaders try to duck out of conversations related to ethics and morality, believing these issues have nothing to do with meeting the company's bottom line. No wonder our kids are confused. No wonder they are lying, stealing, and cheating.

It is easy for us who do not hold nationally recognized positions of leadership to shoot at the inconsistencies and sins of our leaders. It is another thing to remember that these leaders grew up in our neighborhoods, went to our schools, churches, and synagogues, and were raised in our families. Our leaders merely reflect what we the people have become. The moral confusion on the national stage is merely a reflection of the moral confusion that exists in our families, schools, and communities. The reason that many of our kids do not have a moral compass is because many of us did not have one to give to them.

The Imaginary Game of Building Character Apart from Morality

Character is the combination of moral qualities by which a person is judged apart from intellect and talent. It is difficult these days for us to talk in secular contexts about moral qualities, especially in terms of defining the basis of moral behavior. Does morality have its basis in personal preference, cultural mores, universally recognized codes of behavior, or in God-determined moral absolutes, such as the Ten Commandments?

It is very important for us to understand the basis for our moral decision-making. If I make moral decisions based on my own personal preferences and biases, then I must realize that as my preferences and biases change, so too will my views of morality. If I make moral decisions based on the moral absolutes given by God in communiqués such as the Ten Commandments, then I must understand that things such as lying and stealing are always wrong, and that I am accountable not only to myself and my community for moral behavior, but also to God. The latter basis has greater weight of authority and accountability—a greater sense of "oughtness"— than the former.

Character education is one of the hot topics in educational circles today. It is being discussed by by parents and teachers in private schools, parochial schools, and public schools, and by parent/teachers in home schools. This emphasis on character education, which was so much a part of education when our country was founded, is warmly welcomed.[4] It also comes with some concerns.

I believe that in our homes and schools we must teach our kids the basis for morality and not just the actions of morality. If we just teach children examples of moral behavior without clearly explaining why we ought to live morally, we take away the proper motivation. Our kids walk away thinking that moral behavior is largely a matter of personal preference. Character education that does not clearly explain the "oughtness" of morality adds to the confusion about the importance of character and ethical behavior that our kids already experience. As parents, we need to exemplify a life of character through our words and actions. We must also work with our children through the years to help them understand why they must grow up to be men and women of character. They need to learn from us what character looks like and why it is required.

It is also important that parents encourage their local school boards to adopt character education programs. As students in their schools discuss character, it gives them the opportunity to learn how to express their own understanding of its importance. As schools require character reflective behavior of their students, the students learn how to make right choices in a culture that is very different from their home. Though most public schools will stop short of teaching a religious basis for character, there can be great value for our kids to be a part of character education programs. These programs can be an addition to, but not a substitute for, family based character building.

The Source for Psychological Hardiness

A frequently asked question in academic and professional circles these days is: "Are leaders made or born? Is leadership an ability and lifestyle that can be developed through training and practice, or is it largely due to gifting and abilities with which one is born?" The answers to these questions are not as apparent as they may seem.

University of Chicago researchers Suzanne C. Kobasa and Salvatore R. Maddi studied groups of Illinois Bell executives to determine why some executives can endure great amounts of stress and yet not suffer significant physical illness. From their research, they found that the attitudinal quality that distinguished those who endure great stress without physical sickness is the quality of "psychological hardiness."[5] The researchers found that psychological hardiness is more important in dealing with stress than personal constitution, health practices, or social support.[6]

The most important finding from the study describes how this psychological hardiness is developed. "According to researchers, the family atmosphere is the most important breeding ground for a hardy attitude."[7] This study reminds us again of the fundamental importance of the family unit and its ability to shape at the deepest level the hearts and minds of our future leaders. When parents guide children in making and keeping commitments, they are sowing the seeds of hardiness in their children. The same is true when parents require their kids to face rather than avoid difficult challenges and personal fears. Parents also raise psychologically hardy children by leading them to see life as a great opportunity for a purposeful adventure rather than as fearful quest for status quo security. They exemplify and teach their kids the wisdom of Helen Keller's belief that, "Security is mostly a superstition. It does not exist in nature. Life is either a daring adventure or nothing."

Our country is in search of leaders of character, competence, and commitment to lead us in the 21st century. From a long-term perspective, we need look no further than our own homes to see what our leadership prospects are. In families where parents model integrity, kindness, hard work, and respect for others, children grow up understanding character as a lifestyle. Parents who take seriously their responsibilities to plan for their families and to lead their families through the challenges of life teach their children on a daily basis the essence of competence in leadership. As parents and grandparents live out with grace and love their commitments to each other and to their children, they forge into their kid's hearts an orientation toward fulfilling their own commitments.

Our leadership in our businesses, communities, and churches will be misguided if it is not coupled with consistent servant leadership in our families. This family leadership is a life-long learning process where prima donnas and "absenteeism" are not allowed. Leading our families can never be done with perfection, yet it must be pursued with diligence and vigilance. Parents who fail to lead within their families erode the weight of influence that they exert outside of the family

Parents and grandparents who take seriously our country's need for leaders take control of their time and their energy to ensure that they have sufficient time at home, carefully tending to their seedbed of leadership. These parents and grand-parents realize that the most effective solution to our country's dearth of principled leaders is the purposeful nurturing and developing of our chil-dren. Rather than spending hours cursing Washington over endless cups of coffee, they address the current and future needs of our coun-try through the purposeful parenting of those chil-dren that have been entrusted to them.

Chip Steiger in this chapter's opening story realized that his family was a seedbed for leader-ship. Washington had been more than he could handle, at least at his current stage of life. He real-ized that his great opportunity for influence and public service was not in Washington, but in his own backyard. It is my belief that each of us that God has blessed to be parents has the same great opportunity for influence and public service. And if enough of us assume this responsibility, one day Washington will be different.

A Foundation, a Compass, and Fertile Soil

In the precious few years given to parent our children, there are many ways to prepare and equip them. For those parents who want their kids to become lifestyle leaders, there are three impor-tant gifts they can give their them:

- A foundation of right and wrong
- A compass for personal decision-making
- Fertile soil to nurture lifestyle leadership

A Foundation of Right and Wrong

For our kids to build moral authority as a basis for their future leadership, they must develop an awareness of and a respect for right and wrong. The development of this awareness and respect is a complex endeavor that goes far beyond endless lists of rules. Our ultimate goal as parents in this area is not rule-bound conformity, although rules certainly have to be taught. Our goal is that as our kids grow up, they will understand the moral basis for decision-making and the importance to choose what is right. The primary teaching tools parents have are our own examples of moral decision-making and the demonstration of our source of authority from which we derive our understanding of right and wrong.

As lifestyle leaders, we teach our kids as we live. Through our instruction and example, our children will learn the following from our decision-making processes:

1. What authority source we appeal to as the basis for moral decision-making. They will learn if our source of authority comes primarily from our own preferences and biases, the mores of the culture around us, universally recognized codes of behavior, philosophical beliefs, or from God-given moral absolutes.

2. How our primary authority source guides us in making moral decisions; how we handle the many so-called "gray" areas of decision-making, where there is no clear right and wrong.

3. The value of making right choices. They will also evaluate the validity of the authority source from which we derive our understanding of right and wrong.

4. How we confront our failure to always do the right thing. This will be a powerful lesson for them. If we dismiss our own moral failures, large or small, we will teach our children to do the same. As lifestyle leaders, we must realize that we will fail. When we fail, we must take responsibility for our actions, seek forgiveness, and if appropriate, make restitution. One of the great moments in parenting is when we ask our children's forgiveness for wrong choices we make related to them.

As we model moral decision-making for our kids, we establish the basis for instructing them in choosing right and wrong. As I mentioned earlier, I believe when we are teaching our kids right and wrong our lips should persuade and our lives command. Our personal example will speak volumes to our children about how and why a person chooses right over wrong.

A Compass for Personal Decision-making

Our kids need our example, but they also need a compass to take with them when they are on their own. We need to teach them the substance of our authority source and how it gives guidance in moral decision-making. If your source of authority is comprised of your own preferences and biases, then your goal will be to help your kids understand your preferences, your biases, and how they inform you to make moral decisions. If you make moral decisions based upon the mores and nuances of the culture around you, you must teach your kids how to understand cultural expectations, and how to make decisions that reflect the values of the culture. If you believe there is a universal code of moral behavior found in all cultures at all times, then you need to explain this code to your children, then show them how to align their behavior with the dictates of the code. Parents who believe that the authority source for moral decision-making is in the tenets of a particular philosophy must explain the meaning and implications of that philosophy to their kids and show how it gives guidance in everyday life.

Those parents who find their basis for moral decision-making in God-given moral absolutes have a little more work to do with their kids. To fully understand God-given moral codes, such as the Ten Commandments, one has to also understand the faith that these commands exemplify. The Ten Commandments diminish in meaning when extracted from religious faith. To teach our kids the importance of God-given moral codes and the guidance that these codes provide, our children must understand their Author and His purposes. Secular explanations of God-given moral codes can only go so far in establishing the meaning and guidance that comes from them.

Our babies too quickly become first graders and go from us to school each day. Our first graders too quickly become teenagers and engage in activities away from our direct supervision. Our teenagers too quickly become adults and enter into their marriages, families, and careers. While we have them, we must give them a foundation for understanding right and wrong and a compass for personal decision-making. And all along the way, we want to surround them with the fertile soil in which lifestyle leadership flourishes.

Fertile Soil Nurtures Lifestyle Leadership

As parents, we cannot make our kids become what we want. Our children will choose what they become. However, we *can* surround our kids with experiences, lessons, people, discipline, instruction, modeling, love, trust, and feedback—elements that act like fertile soil from which lifestyle leadership will most likely germinate and flourish. As mentioned earlier, it is the parents' example that communicates most powerfully. However, along with the parents' example there must be the intentional provision of other ingredients to further define, exemplify, encourage, and motivate lifestyle leadership and its practice for our kids. We want to give our children every reason to commit and take responsibility for their personal influence. We also want to give them plenty of experiences and lessons as to why they must not merely live for themselves and their own comforts. Furthermore, we want our kids to realize that they can make a positive impact in their sphere of influence, and that becoming a victim to their circumstances is a waste of life. We cannot make our kids believe these things and commit to these practices, especially when they are far away from us. What we can do is surround them with rich and intentional soil that will help foster this kind of development.

A fertile environment can at times be compromised through external contaminants. It is the parents' responsibility to monitor the soil around their children and amend it as necessary. When negative influences come into your kid's life, you should turn these events into learning experiences in which your child learns to use the compass that you have given them. Some influences on your child will need to be confronted or removed by the parent. The parents' responsibility is neither to micromanage their child's environment nor to abandon their child in their environment. Responsible parents must monitor and amend the environment in order to provide the best soil possible for the development of lifestyle leadership in their children.

Training and Influence, Control and Conscience

Parenting is a function of training and influencing that moves from the power of the parent's control to the power of the child's conscience. As the child moves into the teenage years, the parent's role flexes from one of training to one of influencing. The parents' hope is that as they loosen their control during the teenage years, the child's conscience will have developed to the point where it begins to empower the child to make choices that are aligned with a proper set of core beliefs and virtues.

More specifically, during the preteen years parents should focus on life training that builds responsible decision-making and ethical behavior. Parents control most of the daily life of the child and they can use that control to focus the child's attention and development. These are the years during which the parents are slowly, patiently, and incrementally building into the life of the child. In these years parents establish their love, commitment, and trustworthiness to their child. As these important concepts are established in the child and in the parent-child relationship, they form the basis upon which the parents will influence the child in the teenage years.

During the teenage years, parents learn to loosen some (but not all) of their control and focus on influencing their child's decisions and behavior. The practices and beliefs that the parents have established in their children and the quality of relationship that has been built with their children largely determine the degree of influence that they have with their teenagers. Parents should allow their teens to learn more and more lessons because of their decisions. In other words, parents let their teenagers learn from their successes and their mistakes; if their teens make good choices, they enjoy good results; if they make poor choices, they suffer hard consequences. In these years, it is important that parents do not attempt to micromanage their kids or shield them from difficult consequences. It is in the teen years that parents usually begin to see the substance of what they have built in their kids' lives.

One of the things that parents hopefully find in their teenager is a developing conscience that relies on the parent-provided compass to make good decisions. If the child's conscience is developing and the moral compass in place, then parenting in the teenage years can be a great adventure in helping your child move toward responsible adulthood. If the conscience is disengaged and there is no compass, then parenting in the teenage years is a maddening adventure akin to guiding a ship without a rudder. In both circumstances, parenting during the teenage years is an adventure. In the former scenario, it is an adventure that is heading toward a good end. In the latter, it is an adventure into chaos.

Although parents shift from training to influencing and from control to relaxing control, their attention must remain focused throughout these transition years. It is important that teenagers realize that parents are very aware of their condition and are still fully engaged, although perhaps playing different roles. Parents' engagement and focus give teenagers a sense of security and a reminder of healthy boundaries. Many times teenagers will communicate that they do not appreciate their parents' attention or involvement. Parents should not let this kind of rejection cause them to retract from their children. Part of the teenage growing process involves believing that they don't need their parents anymore. Part of responsible parenting involves knowing that as long as you live, there will be a role for you to play in your kids' lives.

So where does Chip begin as he moves back home from Washington and reengages in fathering his sons? He begins by realizing that American culture is giving his sons some confusing messages about morality. He also begins by realizing that his time of training his sons is coming to an end. Chip is moving into the years of *influencing* his sons' decisions and behavior based upon what Claire and he have already built into their lives and upon the relationship that they have established with their kids. These years for Chip and Claire will be a great parenting adventure. If they have built well and gained their sons' trust and love, and if their sons' consciences are empowering them to use the compass that Chip and Claire have given them, then this great parenting adventure has great potential for a happy ending.

8 • Building Great People

Replacing the Ladder with a Hoe

Packing the last box until it was stuffed, Jack sat down at his desk for the last time. He could not believe that his days at Data Services were over. Although he had only been there for six years as Vice President of Operations, it had been six wonderful years, and he had developed many new friendships.

Jack had come to Data Services from one of their competitors that was undergoing a major restructuring. His old company needed to let him go or move him into early retirement, and Data Services was very glad to land someone with his years of experience. Rodney, the CEO of Data Services, was in his late thirties and had recognized that he needed the perspective of a "seasoned old geezer," as Jack called himself. Jack was glad to have had these six years to help firm up the company's operations and productivity.

Jack's mind drifted to the dinner that the company had held for Marge and him the night before. Although he didn't know how to say it to those who attended, the dinner meant the world to him. The senior management team from his old company had surprised him by also attending. When he heard that Data Services was going to host this dinner, Jack's former boss had called Rodney and asked if they could come and honor Jack as well. The Mayor and a number of kids (now adults) who Jack had mentored over the years had also come to honor him. Most importantly, Jack and Marge's three kids, their spouses, and their five grandchildren were there. Their eldest child, Gwen, was called on to give a toast in honor of Jack and Marge. That was one of the highlights of the evening.

When Rodney came to the lectern to close the evening with his remarks, he was visibly moved by the occasion. He spoke generously about Jack's impact on the company's operations. He then focused on Jack's development of the people at Data Services. He spoke candidly about the ways that Jack had influenced his development as a leader. Rodney then shared a number of anecdotes about how others in the company had been positively impacted by Jack's leadership. He then reached behind the curtain and brought out a gold-plated hoe. "Jack, most people believe that they need to climb the ladder to success, even if it means pushing others off as they go," Rodney said. "When I look at you, you don't have a ladder at all—you have a hoe. You quietly and effectively cultivate leadership in those around you, above you, and below you. We want to give you this hoe in appreciation for your investment in our development as leaders. We will also be placing smaller replicas of this hoe on the wall in every manager's office."

Rodney concluded by saying, "Jack, I don't believe that you have ever climbed the ladder to success, and yet you are one of the most successful business leaders that I have ever known. You did not need a ladder to succeed, all you needed was a hoe."

As Jack shook himself out of his memories and carried the last box from his office to his car, he wondered where his next place of service would be. He didn't really believe in retirement. He looked at the next phase of his life as an opportunity to help people develop without all of the disruptions that came from his job. With hoe in hand, he looked forward to finding the next place that needed a "seasoned old geezer."

A Career or an Investment?

"The real test of a man is not how well he plays the role he has invented for himself, but how well he plays the role that destiny assigned to him." Vaclav Havel.[1] When I was a young man fresh out of college, one of my mentors challenged me with the following question, "Do you want to spend your life or invest it?" As I now look back on the years of my life, I believe that this was one of the most important questions I was ever asked. I decided that I wanted to invest my life, especially in helping others accomplish their purposes. Borrowing from Robert Frost's "The Road Not Taken," that decision has "made all the difference."[2]

Jack in the opening story is a great example of a man who chose to invest his life. He succeeded in his career, rising to the position of Senior Vice President. But much more importantly, he invested his life in the development of others. Because of this investment, the years of his career were not just spent; these years were invested and yielded a crop of current and future leaders at Data Services and at the other companies where he worked. Jack's job was not just a means for his advancement, success, and financial security, although these are legitimate endeavors. His job was also a vast garden in which he cultivated leadership in others.

The Selfishness of the Great "American" Dream
We have perhaps the greatest opportunity for personal advancement that has ever existed in history. With this opportunity comes a dream of financial security, property ownership, and personal freedom—the Great "American" Dream, which is really a universal dream. As great as this dream is, I do not believe that it should be understood as a goal, but rather as a means. Accomplishing the Great Dream allows us the opportunity and ability to be of greater service to others. Attaining financial security, property ownership, and personal freedom without using these achievements as a means for service to others is largely a form of self-indulgence. Moreover, these pieces of the Great Dream will grow increasingly

meaningless if they are grubbed and clenched rather than used and shared.

Another problem with the Great Dream is that it predominately satisfies only the materialistic aspect of our nature. At the core of our being, we long to be loved and to have meaningful relationships. This need is ultimately met through our relationship with God. It is also met through our loved ones around us to whom we commit. The Great Dream will satisfy our desire for money, possessions, and freedom. However, if these three things are attained apart from meaningful relationships, we have accomplished our goals—but no one around us cares. We become ensnared in the trappings of the Great Dream, all the while missing the most important things in life.

We are blessed with the opportunity to pursue the Great Dream. In our pursuits, however, we must remember that there is a danger to the dream—the danger of becoming self-absorbed and self-indulgent. The great opportunity of the dream is that in attaining it, we have greater freedom and resources by which to be a blessing to others. In blessing others, even after our deaths, our lives will speak and influence. In becoming self-absorbed and self indulgent, we live to ourselves and die to ourselves. The Great Dream is a great privilege that in itself will never fully satisfy us.

An Investment into the Lives of Others

There are several principles that most of us use in making financial investments. These principles include the following ideas:

1. Invest with hopes of future, significant returns.
2. Do not place all of your investment dollars in one stock; spread your money around.
3. Invest in companies that you have reason to believe have great promise. Sometimes this hope is based on past performance, and sometimes it is based on calculations about the future.
4. Part of the return on your investment is intended not for yourself, but for your loved ones.

Let's see how these principles apply to investing in others. By investing in others, I mean giving some of your time, expertise, resources, and attention to someone else with hope that you can help that person progress in accomplishing their life purpose. Investing can be done in informal ways, such as end-of–the-day conversations, or in more formal ways, such as mentoring and coaching. In this definition of investing in others, there is the hope for development to a desired future position beyond the "investee's" current position. This fits with principle one above regarding hopes for future significant returns. As we invest our time, expertise, resources, and attention in people, it is with the hope that we will positively impact others' lives. It is also with the hope that those we invest in will in turn invest their new knowledge in others.

As a principle, it is best to invest your time, expertise, resources, and attention with several people at a time. Just as you shouldn't put all of your money in one stock, you should steer away from investing in only one person. For whatever reasons, the investment in the person's life may fail. They may not choose to use the investment as a means for growth, rather choosing to waste your efforts. Spreading your investments amongst several people helps prevent the disappointment of failed investments, and prevents your interest and efforts from being wasted or abused.

As with any major endeavor, begin slowly and carefully. Invest a little in the beginning of your investment relationship to see what your protégé does with your efforts. If he or she uses your investment as a means for personal growth, then you can confidently invest more. If they waste or ignore your investment, you should investigate the lack of responsiveness before you invest more.

This leads to the third principle of investing, which states that you invest in those who you believe have great promise. Great promise is exemplified by an eagerness to grow and enough humility to learn. It also means that your potential protégés' personal values include helping others and not just themselves. Your career will provide a great fishing pond where you can catch people of great promise in which to invest. If they are not yet ready for someone to invest in their lives, throw them back in and let them grow a little more. During the course of your life, you will only have the time, expertise, resources, and attention to invest in relatively few people. You want to make sure that you invest in those who have promise of good returns.

The fourth principle of investing states that part of the return on your investment is intended not for yourself, but for your loved ones. This tenet is especially true when investing in the lives of others. When you invest in the lives of others, very little of the return comes to you. Most of the return goes to the one in which you invested, and then to the people he or she benefits as a result of your investment. Stephen Covey has reminded us of the adage, "Give a man a fish, and you feed him for a day. Teach him how to fish, and you feed him for a lifetime."[3] The reason you take the time to teach others to fish is not so that they can bring you fish. You already know how to fish. You teach them so they can provide for themselves and share with those around them. You also teach in the hopes that they will share their new knowledge by teaching it to others. The return on your investment multiplies, compounding with each person provided for and each new fisherperson braving the water. The benefit may not directly affect you, but it definitely affects others. Your return comes from the joy of knowing you have changed the world by investing your life and not merely spending it.

Great Leaders Build Great People

A critical test separates effective leaders from legendary leaders. This test takes place within leaders when they begin to question the message and legacy of their life. What is the message of their life and leadership? What legacy are they leaving behind for others to ponder and learn from?

Sadly enough, many leaders never ask these questions, much less answer them. The busyness of life and work, the fears that gnaw within and drive them meaninglessly forward, rob them of moments of reflection. By cooperating as willing partners in this theft of reflection, they demonstrate that they are ever wary of taking an honest, deep look within. These are the men and women of leadership who accomplish much, but influence little.

Fortunately, in every generation there are those leaders who decide to face the questions of meaning and message. These are the leaders who commit to the roles that destiny has prepared for them. In choosing to define and play out their roles, they quickly realize that their leadership should not be recognized for its organizational or fiscal accomplishments alone. They believe that the core of legendary leadership consists of human influence.

Legendary leaders focus not just on what is happening to the bottom line, but also on what is happening to people. They ask, "What are we becoming?" as well as "What are we accomplishing?" These leaders realize that generous monetary compensation is important, but that it has limited effect in building and sustaining ethical choices.

These questions and beliefs guide their actions because they want those they lead to be improved by their leadership. These leaders determine not to use their followers or coddle them, but rather to help them to be better, more ethical people.

A commitment to ethical influence is nurtured or negated by the life of the leader. His or her speech and actions in both public and private contexts will determine if their ethical influence carries any weight. Leaders who endeavor to build their moral influence choose to live exemplary lives because it is the right thing to do, and because it is a prerequisite to positively influencing others.

In exerting ethical influence, leaders should move purposefully, slowly, and with genuine humility. Their aim is not to coerce ethical responses, but rather to encourage and support ethical choices. These leaders must be quick to face their own failings and yet not sheepishly hide behind them. Their lives, with both strengths and weaknesses, must become one of their most powerful assets.

Legendary leaders are not merely "nice people getting nicer." These leaders are people who wrestle well with their own ethical weaknesses and who, by their words and actions, encourage others to do the same. In so doing, they effectively demonstrate why they choose ethical behavior and how it shapes their lives. They speak first from their examples and secondly with their voices.

Leaders who exert legendary influence do so in an active, intentional fashion. They are committed to playing their role in building better people. This role must be played with humility and sensitivity, but not with passivity. Legendary leaders do not merely *hope* to be persons of ethical influence; they *intentionally learn* how to be persons of ethical influence.

Six principles form the foundation of ethical influence. These principles serve as reference points for leadership decisions throughout life and in every leadership context. Leaders who exert ethical influence relearn and reapply these principles as their experiences, knowledge, and responsibilities expand.

1. Ethical influence flows from those who align their speech and behavior with transcendent ethical core beliefs and virtues.
2. Encouraging ethical development in others occurs in a context of freedom that involves growth, discussion, and disagreement.
3. Leaders must learn to creatively and meaningfully affirm ethical behavior in others without building cliques within the organization.
4. Blatant unethical behavior must be confronted.
5. The leader must never request or manipulate unethical behavior from those that they lead.
6. The chief textbook on ethical influence must be the life of the leader. Their life must transparently communicate the results and the challenges of ethical living.

The opportunity to manifest greatness always exists for leaders. This greatness always involves working with people to accomplish worthy goals. The secret ingredient of leadership greatness is ethical influence. It is this type of leadership that produces not only great accomplishments, but also great people.

This opportunity for greatness is available to all leaders who vigilantly build their own lives into wellsprings of ethical influence. Instead of being remembered as a person who accomplished much and influenced little, the leader will be remembered by those who followed as a treasured mentor who served as a guide to successful living.

Mentoring that Builds Leadership

Great leadership requires great influence. Great leaders are not born with a genetic proclivity toward great leadership, nor are they solely self-made into great leaders. A study of any honorable and effective leader will show that during their development, the leader received many infusions of substantive influence from relationships and events that they experienced. Emerging leaders use great influences to help them become great leaders.

At a time when Americans have compelling reasons for concern about the current and future leadership of our country, we must consider the necessity of becoming a source of great influence. There is more to be done than sitting, listening to "talk radio," and picking our current leaders apart. Our young employees are in their developmental years for becoming leaders in their marriages, families, careers, and communities. Ours is a context for proactive influence, not reactive cynicism.

But where does one begin? Great influence that builds great leadership is a mentoring process. Mentoring that builds leadership must be based upon an understanding of how leadership development takes place. As you come to understand how leaders develop, you can understand how to support and encourage this process.

In their practical, research-based book, *The Leadership Challenge*, authors James Kouzes and Barry Posner describe the practices and commitments of effective leaders. The book's last chapter, "Becoming a Positive Force," gives direction to the development of effective leadership. The authors state that, from their studies of thousands of leaders, they have gleaned three experiences from which people learn to lead. Their findings have been confirmed by similar studies done by the Center for Creative Leadership and by the Honeywell Corporation.[4]

The three experiences that help people learn to lead, listed in order of importance, are:
- Trial and error
- Observation of others
- Education[5]

Trial and error occurs as emerging leaders receive leadership responsibilities and wrestle with accomplishing these responsibilities. Young leaders learn practical skills and insights as they observe other leaders fulfilling their leadership responsibilities. Education for developing leaders can occur in traditional classroom settings as well as in experiential learning environments.

These three leadership-learning experiences suggest three services that mentors can provide for the development of emerging leaders:

- Guidance
- Facilitation
- Input

By providing these services for their protégés, mentors can speed their protégés' leadership development processes and help ensure the quality of their development. Just as a catalyst in a chemical reaction causes the reaction to take place more quickly and effectively, so a mentor has the potential to trigger and expedite their protégé's leadership development process.

Guidance

As leaders-in-the-making learn by trial-and-error, observation of others and educational opportunities, they have great need for various forms of guidance. At times, the protégé will need guidance that gives *direction* through the maze of leadership decisions and challenges. At other times, when the leadership context seems fast-paced, chaotic, and ethically challenging, the protégé needs guidance on the *meaning* of principled leadership that is both effective and ethically balanced.

At regular intervals, developing leaders also need guidance that fosters courage for decisive action and moral integrity. They need mentors whose words and actions model the way for courageous steps forward. Finally, protégés need *feedback* that guides them as they apply the lessons learned from their trial and error, observation of others, and educational opportunities.

Without guidance from a mentor, most emerging leaders go through their development processes lacking the necessary wisdom to learn readily and effectively. These developing leaders tend to need longer exposure to the three primary learning experiences to learn the same lessons those with mentors learn more quickly and easily. Without the catalytic guidance of a mentor, the leadership development process takes more time to produce the same results.

Facilitation

Mentors can also serve their protégés by facilitating relationships and learning experiences for them. The mentor facilitates these relationships and experiences by using their influence and networks to provide learning opportunities for the protégé.

The mentor facilitates *strategic leadership experiences* that stretch and challenge the protégé to foster growth through trial and error. The mentor's goal is to provide broad leadership experiences that require focused commitment, and that at times may end in failure. These experiences build toughness, confidence, and breadth of leadership knowledge, and thus are invaluable to any developing leader.

Emerging leaders need to observe role models and build relationships with other leaders.

Mentors facilitate this observation of others by facilitating *relationships with exemplars and comrades.* Through their influence and network of relationships, the mentor can introduce and assign their protégés to people from whom they can learn valuable aspects of the art of leadership.

The educational needs of the protégé include classroom instruction and hands-on training. Mentors can help meet these needs by providing *access to proven educational opportunities.* Protégés often need seasoned direction as to what educational opportunities they should pursue. Committed mentors use their influence and networks to connect their protégés with appropriate opportunities for instruction and training.

Emerging leaders who do not have the help of a mentor focused on facilitation are at a disadvantage because of their own limited influence and networks. They have to find their own way down the path of leadership development. Like those emerging leaders who do not have a mentor's guidance, those without a mentor's facilitation take longer to make their way down the road, and possibly learn less in the process.

Input

Seasoned mentors who know their protégés well can substantively address their instructional and training needs. In this role, the mentor is a provider of wise input that specifically meets the needs of the protégé. The mentor serves by giving customized educational opportunities to the developing leader.

The mentor's input generally focuses on four learning areas. The first area is *knowledge*, which has to do with basic leadership concepts and content. Second, the mentor focuses on the *skills* needed for effective long-term leadership. A successful mentor also gives input related to the kind of *character* required for balanced effective leadership. Finally, the mentor provides input about the protégé's development of compelling *vision*.

Contributions from the mentor provide customized assistance to the protégé, which also can shorten the leadership development process. Those emerging leaders who do not have the input of a mentor usually learn from generalized and generic education and training opportunities. The limited effect of this on their development is obvious.

The Impact of these Services

These three services—guidance, facilitation, and input—should, on a long-term basis, only be given to those who will put into action what they have received. Mentoring of this kind requires a sacrifice on the part of the mentor, and the protégé should recognize the mentor's efforts as a precious investment. However, even excellent mentoring is not a magic formula guaranteeing effective leadership development. It is, as was stated above, a catalyst that helps the leadership development process occur at a more rapid and effective pace.

With the great concerns held about the current and future leadership of our country, it is extremely important for us to remember that great leadership requires great influence. In the sphere of influence provided by our careers, it is our privilege to provide the guidance, facilitation, and input that our emerging leaders need. In so doing, we gain the blessing of serving well in the honorable role of mentor.

Breathing on the Coals of the Heart

It is said that human capacity is a state of mind. Although this may be true, the heart most often controls the expansion of one's capacity. Moving to a higher level of performance usually requires a person to face and choose against an area of fear in the heart. This concept has immense value to leadership in today's organizations.

Current corporate trends move toward either small organizations whose future existence is often uncertain or behemoth mergers whose profitability is often uncertain. In either scenario, there is increased pressure upon employees to stretch their capacities to higher levels. In organizations where people are genuinely valued and developed, this pressure can have a very positive effect on those involved. In organizations that do not value and develop their people, the effect is usually demeaning and demoralizing.

Leaders committed to the people they lead play a key role in the positive expansion of their constituents' capacities. One of the ways a leader accomplishes this is by understanding the relationship between fear and capacity. A leader's constituents must wrestle with the fears that hold them back in order to make the breakthroughs needed for the team's success. Wise leaders learn to recognize the fears that limit the capacity and performance of their immediate followers. Often times, leaders learn to identify these fears in others by first identifying them in their own hearts.

As they come to understand the fears that control the human heart, leaders are able to communicate to their people the need for courageous choices in the midst of gripping fear. In so doing, the leader breathes on the coals of the follower's heart to re-ignite the courage that fear had chilled. As the fire of these coals brings warmth again, an increased willingness to believe that one's capacities can expand to meet new challenges grows. An understanding of the true nature of courage—voiced by Mark Twain as, "Courage is resistance to fear, mastery of fear, not absence of fear"—also develops in the heart of the follower.[6]

Leaders breathe on the coals of the heart by positively encouraging their followers to make the following choices:
- Risk over stability
- Collaboration over isolation
- Growth over comfort
- A noble effort over a routine performance

Choosing Risk over Perceived Stability

True risk always presents the possibility of real loss, and so many people choose perceived stability over risk out of a fear of loss. However, living in unending stability is not a real possibility. As Max Depree says well, "Risk is like change, it's not a choice."[7]

Choosing Collaboration over Isolation

People choose isolation over collaboration because of a fear of loosing control. Increasing one's performance in many of today's organizations requires a commitment to work more effectively in team contexts. This requirement strikes deep in the hearts of those who fear loosing control of all aspects of processes and outcomes.

Choosing Growth over Comfort

People choose comfort over growth because of a fear of facing personal ignorance or inadequacy. Those who choose to grow and learn face the fact that they do not possess all the skills and knowledge they need. These seekers must recognize that they may fail in their pursuit of new knowledge and abilities. Yet they also realize that to perform at a higher level, they cannot remain in the "safe" world of their comfort zone.

Choosing Noble Effort over Routine Performance

People often choose a routine performance over a noble effort because of a fear of public ridicule. They fear that others will laugh at their zealous attempts to give a 110 percent contribution to the mission of the organization. Staying in the pack of status quo performers has the appearance of secure anonymity. However, the competitiveness of today's corporate contexts increasingly weeds out routine performers. There is however a more important reason than job security for us to encourage others to choose a noble effort. A lifetime of routine performance is a life wasted rather than an adventure lived. It is in reaching for accomplishments beyond our current abilities that we move out of our comfort zone and into the adventure of achieving more than we could have ever imagined.

The Source of Encouragement

Encouragement that breathes on the coals of the heart and loosens the grip of fear must have two ingredients. This kind of support must flow from a life that is marked by integrity. It is difficult to gain courage from someone who is not facing his or her own fears. It is also difficult to gain courage from someone whose life is ethically compromised. The quality of the leader's life is a great determinant in the depth of the leader's influence.

Second, this kind of encouragement must flow from a life that has taken the time and made the effort to understand the constituents' challenges. People are demeaned and demoralized when their leader's attempts at encouragement have the platitudinous sound of "Buck up, little camper." Those who seek first to understand gain an opening into others' lives in which to provide real encouragement.

On a daily basis, today's leaders must inspire greater performances and better results from fewer constituents with fewer resources. Leaders who use real encouragement to breathe on the coals of the heart begin the process that can result in the positive expansion of their constituents' capacities. This effort can also help the leader understand how positive, life-driven motivation works. Both of these results are greatly needed.

We should look at our working lives as a time to hoe rather than climb. Few opt for the hoe, and our world suffers because of it. Jack reminds us that when it is all over, those who have skillfully used the hoe have gained—and given—the most. It is a choice between spending your life and investing it.

9 · As Iron Sharpens Iron

The Inestimable Value of Good Friends

It was a conversation that came too early and ended too soon. Two men, two friends, were awkwardly telling each other goodbye. John had flown out to Phoenix to visit Ken under the pretense of seeing Ken in his world. While there, John met Ken's friends and co-workers and had a great visit with Ken's family. However, the real reason John came was to tell his friend of 20 years that this would be their last time together. He had terminal cancer. Throughout the visit his pain and weakness was a constant reminder of the conversation that they needed to have before John went home.

But how do you begin such a conversation? How do you tell one of your best friends that you will miss him? How do you tell him that you are a better man because of the friendship that you have shared? How do you explain all that you have learned from each other? How do you tell him how deeply you ache over leaving your wife and four children alone once you die? How do you talk about the transition plans that your firm is already beginning to ensure seamless profitability despite your "abrupt departure?" How do you let the conversation come to its inevitable end when you want it to go on for many more years?

While John and Ken basked in the warm September sun, the conversation began. First came the facts, which were followed by the standard expressions of hope and optimism. Finally, the two friends stopped talking, looked at each other, and realized what they really wanted to say. They wanted to say thank you. From the day that they met in college, their friendship had been a wonderful blending of two very different men. They had challenged, competed, and learned from each other. Sometimes they disliked one another. As the years of their friendship grew, they increasingly became trusted friends and advisors to one another. They both had great aspirations for the kind of men, husbands, fathers, and professionals they wanted to become. Through their interactions and commitment to each other, they were unobtrusively helping the other become the man he wanted to be. And so, now that their conversation was ending, all they knew to say to each other was thank you. That was all that needed to be said.

As the taxi pulled up to take John to the airport, they hugged each other goodbye. Ken knew that he would never see John again in this life. He also knew that as long as he lived, he would never forget their conversation. As the years since John's death have come and gone, Ken thinks of him often and visits his grave when he can. And every time he does, all he needs to say is thank you.

Two Are Better Than One
The Peril of Isolation

> *Two are better than one, because they have a good return for their work:*
> *If one falls down, his friend can help him up.*
> *But pity the man who falls and has no one to help him up!*
> *Also, if two lie down together, they will keep warm. But how can one keep warm alone?*
> *Though one may be overpowered, two can defend themselves.*
> *A cord of three strands is not quickly broken.*[1]
> Ecclesiastes 4:9-12

"Whatever Happened To Friendship" is the title of an intriguing *Wall Street Journal* article. In it, Nancy Ann Jeffrey makes the following observation:

> While countless companies have become more family friendly—even letting workers bring their pets to the office—friendship isn't on the radar screen. Instead, the importance of spending time with friends is played down as an optional indulgence that steals scarce hours out of an already jam-packed schedule.[2]

When friendships become an optional indulgence, a great source of life perspective and balance is lost. Lifestyle leaders cannot take the risk of isolating themselves from friends.

Isolation is too often one of the perks that comes with management promotion. As Carol Hymowitz observes, "The biggest jolt for most managers as they climb several rungs up the corporate ladder isn't the bigger risks and added responsibilities. It's the isolation. Not only do they have fewer peers to turn to for counsel and camaraderie, they may be several layers removed from staffers they once talked to several times a day and thought of as colleagues."[3] A problem with many corporate ladders is that on your way up, you can leave many important friends behind.

Isolation from friends is not just a career phenomenon. The pace of American family life similarly challenges the possibility of maintaining long-term friendships. In most dual-income or single-parent families, the hope is that each week there will be time for the family. Friendships outside of the family seem impossible. And yet, the support and encouragement that friendship gives to harried spouses and parents is important in facing the challenges of marriage and parenting. Marriage and family are too important to be compromised because of a lack of outside perspective.

We each have the potential of living in ruts of which we are unaware. These ruts can be a result of our own ignorance, fears, failures, or adversity. Without the perspective and help of friends who live outside our routines, we are more likely to live trapped in our patterns and miss the adventure meant for us. Perspective is not possible in a rut; the walls are too narrow and the furrow too deep. Isolation from friends can mean that we and some of those nearest to us may waste years of our life living in comfortable but misguided ruts.

Another peril of isolation from friends is exposed when calamity or tragedy enters our world. When we fail in our leadership, suffer the loss of a loved one, endure the pain of a wayward teenager, or undergo a financial reversal, where do we go? Or more correctly, to whom do we go? There are times in life when we plainly need help. Even in great marriages, there are times when we need help beyond that which our spouses can give us. We need the help of friends. As the *Book of Ecclesiastes* reminds us, "But pity the man who falls and has no one to help him up!" It is a real pity if we have so isolated ourselves from our friends that we have no one to call when our world, our leadership, or our family begins to unravel.

Lifestyle leadership is all about intentional principled living that establishes the power and effectiveness of our influence in others' lives. A few good friends can be of inestimable value to those who seek to be lifestyle leaders. Friends draw us out of our ruts and come along side when our world goes upside down. Isolation from friends can be a perilous context in which to live and lead. We all need a few good friends.

The Impact of Having a Few Good Friends

I once asked a college student about his best friend. As we discussed their friendship, I asked further, "What would be the net effect to you if your friendship with this friend continued for the next 25 years?" The student's response was striking: "I would live those 25 years continually reminded of what it is that I want to become." Good friends, through their commitment, speech, actions, and examples, remind us of who we aspire to become. "As iron sharpens iron, so one man sharpens another."[4] In the chaotic, warp-speed world in which most leaders live, we need to be reminded early and often about what we want to become. We need friends who know us well enough to know what we aspire to be and to do, and who will take, or make, opportunities to remind us.

Most often, to have great friends, we must learn to be a great friend. This forces us out of our little worlds and into the world of another. It also stretches our hearts beyond ourselves and those immediately around us in order to love someone that may not be much like us or a part of our daily life. Being a great friend pushes us to see life more broadly than we would normally see it. Moving out of our world and into another allows us to reenter our daily lives with fresh perspective of the reality that exists beyond our routines. The cost of friendship is real; the perspective it yields is invaluable.

Good friends impact us all the way to our core. We all have a longing for committed, unmerited loyalty. We want people in our lives who will commit their loyalty to us not because we always deserve it or have always earned it, but just because they care about us. We long for unmerited favor. Ultimately we can only find this in God's perfect love for us. Nevertheless, in our marriages and friendships we hope that we will receive loyalty and favor that commits to us regardless of our successes and failures. And when we are given this gift and we receive it, it gives us the support and courage to risk being the person and leader that we know we ought to be. One of the great possibilities of great friendships is that through them, we can become better men or women than we would be isolated from those friendships.

Long-term Leaders Need Lifelong Friends

Effective long-term leaders need regular infusions of perspective and balance. Without it, tunnel vision and the distortion of imbalance sets in. I believe that one of the competencies that lifestyle leaders must put forward is the ability over time to maintain personal perspective and balance. If leaders are unable to do this, they will eventually crumble under the weight of their leadership, misuse people in order to hide their loss of perspective and balance, or redefine their purposes in order to gain a so-called "success" in spite of their loss of balance and perspective. None of these approaches exemplifies principled leadership.

In order to live and lead with perspective and balance throughout the years, we need a few friends who know our history. And when these friends speak to us, we need to listen. As the ancient wisdom reminds us, "Better is a poor but wise youth than an old but foolish king, who will no longer take advice."[5] Long-term leaders need friends who will serve as wellsprings of perspective and balance. And from this spring leaders should drink deep and often. Wasting the resource of friendship, or worse yet, isolating ourselves from it, is a foolish choice that serves no one.

The Daily Need for 'InCouragement'

We tend to understand encouragement as something that only the weak and downtrodden need, or as superficial patronization. When thinking of encouragement we quickly call up phrases like, "Buck up, little camper," or images of young children having their "boo-boos" kissed and bandaged so that they can run back out and play. Or perhaps we think that encouragement is meaningless flattery and baseless hopefulness conveyed by someone who neither knows us or our current challenges. For many, admitting a need for encouragement would be the ultimate embarrassment; and receiving encouragement would be the ultimate insult.

To properly understand encouragement and our perennial need for it, we must first understand the concept of courage. Courage is derived from the Latin word *cor*, which means heart. We could understand the word encouragement as meaning putting heart into someone, or to give heart to someone. A current definition of the word courage is: "mental or moral strength to venture, persevere, withstand danger, fear, or difficulty."[6] To encourage means that we come along side someone and understand their challenges, fears, and weaknesses, as well as their beliefs and aspirations. We then do what we can to give them the courage to face their challenges, fears, and weaknesses and to live according to their beliefs and aspirations. If we disagree with their beliefs and aspirations, we tell them. However, our goal is not to fix them so that they will be just like us. Our goal is to give them courage to be the person that God wants them to be and to pursue the adventure to which He has called them. Our motivation in all of this is a love that we freely give to them. Our position is that each day we ourselves need encouragement just as much as those to whom we offer it do.

Specifically, I believe that we need to give and receive encouragement in the following areas on a regular basis.

To Choose Against Compromise

In life and long-term leadership, compromise is an ever-present temptation. Compromising our beliefs, our aspirations, our team's mission, vision, and values, and our relationships are temptations that often make sense in the moment but appear foolish and destructive with the perspective of time. A friend's probing question, appeal to conscience, or reminder of who we really want to be can often give us the perspective to remember the danger of compromise and to stand against it.

To Remember the Vision

Great leadership, whether in our marriage, family, or career, helps others see, further define, and pursue a substantive vision. If there is no vision, there is no purpose in leadership. Over time, the leader and those she leads can begin to substitute focus on activity for focus on the vision. The vision dissipates and leadership dissolves into managing activity. At these times, great friends come along side us and help us remember the vision and recommit ourselves to its fulfillment. They spark within us the courage that we need to suspend our busyness and rethink our effectiveness.

To Join Together

An age-old formula for defeat is divide and conquer. When divided from collaboration with like-hearted friends and left to make it on our own, we enter a potential trap that seals our long-term demise. Great friends remind us of our need to join together whenever possible in our work, our challenges, our faith, and our growth. Two really are better than one. We need the strength that comes from joining together with our friends to counteract our tendencies and our culture's pull toward isolation.

To See Reality as It Is

"Face reality as it is, not as it was or as you wish it were."[7] This admonition from Jack Welch, former Chairman and CEO of General Electric Corporation is one of his "Six Rules for Corporate Change." Welch's admonition to corporate leaders is applicable and important for any leader. As life and leadership continue through the years, all of us collect fears, failures, hurts, and blind spots that diminish our ability to face reality as it is. Trusted friends have the opportunity to help us see those parts of reality that we are unwilling or unable to see, or those things of which we are simply ignorant. As we seek out their perspectives on our situations and our leadership, we see beyond ourselves and our protective biases; we gain much needed insight and clarity. Perspective is a precious commodity. Great friends help us to gain perspective and then take action in accordance with reality.

To Take a Break

Sometimes we are too busy digging ourselves into a hole to take a break. When we finally finish the hole, we don't need a break because we are already resting, permanently, in our finely dug grave. Friends help us to see when we need to step back and take a few deep breaths, go on a long drive away from the city, take a weekend off, or go away for two weeks with our spouse and without laptops, pagers, PDA's, and cell phones. Many times we do not realize that we are mentally, physically, emotionally, or spiritually drained; we cannot see that our buckets are empty. Close friends ask the probing questions and make the wise observations that help us see that we really are spent. Through their perspective we realize that we have no more to give because we have given all that we have. They graciously encourage us to put down the shovel, crawl out of the hole, and rest. Upon our return, we are amazed at how we could have spent so much time digging that hole. Friends help us get out of the hole-digging business and into the living and leading business.

To Fully Engage

Friends help us know when it is time to take a break. But they also help us know when it is time to suck it up, go after it, and endure no matter what comes our way. Once a team I lead suffered a public attack on our credibility that was devastating to all of us involved. In discussing this with a friend, I told him that I was ready to walk away and pursue a position in another area. My friend looked at me and said, "John, you have been bucked off the horse, and you need to get back on and ride it." His response was not only the opposite of what I was thinking, it was the last thing that I wanted to hear him say. As I look back at this situation 20 years later, I can see that my friend's counsel to stay engaged, to "get back on the horse and ride it," was sage advice that kept me on track.

There are times when we want to give up, when we want to "try" to do something rather than commit to doing it. There are times when we want to mindlessly stay busy rather than strategically pursue the mission, vision, and values of our organization and lead our people to do the same. In these times we need to reengage our minds, our emotions, our strength, our spirits, and our will. It is our responsibility to do so. It certainly helps if we have the perspective, encouragement, and belief of a friend to help us see what we need to do and to do it. Sometimes we need to get back on the horse and ride it. Friends point us to the horse and help us put our feet back in the stirrups.

To Choose Honor and Wisdom, Not Expediency and Foolishness

Persons of honor live according to boundaries that others either do not recognize or to which they are unwilling to yield. These boundaries establish speech and actions that are appropriate for honorable behavior and those that are not. Examples of such boundaries are as small as opening doors for others and as large as a husband never meeting in private with someone of the opposite sex. As we all know, it is easier to define what honorable behavior looks like than it is to consistently make honorable decisions. The erosion of expedient and foolish decisions can turn each of us honorable "wannabes" into honorable "has beens."

Principled leaders learn the importance of living according to the wisdom that they have gained from their faith, their beliefs, and the lessons they have learned in the course of life. They realize that as they go on in life and leadership, one of the most valuable gifts they can give to others is the wisdom they have earned and by which have lived throughout the years. Expedient and foolish decisions can undermine a life that has otherwise been built upon wise choices. Only a few unwise decisions can bring into question the wisdom and credibility of a lifetime. The daily challenge of living according to honor and wisdom is great. Our daily choices comprise the proving ground upon which our honor and wisdom are established.

In the daily challenge of making honorable and wise decisions, it is of great help to have friends around us who encourage us to make right choices. It is also of great help to have friends around us whose examples remind us of what honor and wisdom look like and what long-term benefits they hold. Lifestyle leadership has no real meaning or value if it is detached from honorable decisions. These decisions require mental and moral strength; they require courage. Having friends that know us and are committed to us can be an invaluable asset when we are making hard choices.

You may ask, "Where do you find great friends?" I believe that you find great friends by seeking to be a great friend. As is true in other areas of life, greatness attracts greatness. As you prove yourself to be a great friend, you draw those who will make the same commitment to you. As you commit to encourage others in the above-mentioned seven areas, you will over time reap what you have sown. Gaining great friends requires the courage and commitment to be a great friend. In other words, it requires an investment.

The Investment

Great friendships require an investment that some, for various reasons, choose not to make. Others willingly make the investment that friendships require because of their need to have friends and their desire to be a friend. These people see their need to love and to be loved, to help and to be helped, to encourage and to be encouraged. There are at least five investments or commitments that friends have to make in order for their friendships to be substantive.

Investment of Time

Friendships take time, although not always great amounts of time. It only takes a few minutes to send an e-mail, make a phone call, write a note, say a prayer, order a book, or reconsider a recent conversation. It also only takes a few minutes a day, perhaps while driving, to think through a friend's current challenges and to determine if there are ways that you can be of help. Similarly, it only takes a few minutes a day to think through your own challenges and decide to communicate them to your friend.

There are moments when a large investment of time is needed. When a marriage is in trouble, a teenager has run away, a company is downsizing, or a cancer exam comes back positive, your friend needs your friendship. You do all that you can to be there for them. You can't (and shouldn't) shoulder the whole load for them. But you should do all that you can because you are their friend.

Investment of Thought

Friendships require purposeful thought about each other's challenges and opportunities. Whenever friends communicate, they receive fresh data that they later think about or "chew on." In their thinking, they are trying to understand and gain insight about their friend's needs. It is a great compliment when you say to your friend, "I've given a lot of thought about what you said the last time we were together. Here are some insights that I've come up with." Jotting down a few things to think about while you are commuting or taking your afternoon walk is an easy way to remember to think about your friend and his current challenges and opportunities.

Investment of Vulnerability and Honesty

Posturing, flattering, and ignoring the proverbial elephant in the living room have no place in great friendships. To be a good friend means that you will vulnerably and honestly tell your story to your friend. You may rightfully choose to not tell your friend every dark detail of your life. But what you do share must always be honest, and must be representative of all of who you are. You must share your thoughts and feelings regularly. You shouldn't expect your friend to drag out of you what is going on in your spheres of influence. You should rather make the details of your life and leadership readily available.

In being a friend you risk the vulnerability of being honest, and the possibility of rejection. Your honesty is required when you reveal who you are, as well as who you find your friend to be. Your honesty is also required when you describe how you see your friend's challenges and opportunities. The purpose for your honesty and vulnerability is not to be a busybody, an uninvited advisor, or a burden. It is rather for the service of your friend. Your involvement should be measured according to your friend's openness and receptivity to your efforts.

Investment of Resources

There are times when monetary costs are involved in a committed friendship. Celebrating birthdays, paying airfare to spend a day catching up with each other, sending a book that might provide insight, and sharing meals all have their costs. However, over the years of a friendship the expenses seem increasingly small. The costs involved in being a faithful friend comprise a sound investment that will bring dividends in both of your lives.

Each of us has limited resources to invest in a friendship. Our commitment to our spouses and families precede our commitment to our friends. For some, this leaves little money at the end of the month to invest in a friendship. Thankfully, there are other resources that we have to invest. Acts of service, words of encouragement, and offering our talents and prayer are non-monetary resources that we can invest in a friendship. Sometimes these gifts mean much more than anything we could ever buy.

The Investment of Large-heartedness

In great friendships there is a commitment to keep pettiness and small-heartedness from entering the relationship. Unwarranted criticism, bickering, and resentment slowly dissolve a great friendship. As the years of a friendship advance, we become increasingly aware of our friends' weaknesses, warts, and idiosyncrasies. Just as in any great marriage, throughout the years we must choose to freely and fully love our friends. Increased familiarity over time can breed pettiness, "score-keeping," and small-heartedness. This can choke out a friendship. One of the most important investments we can make in our friendships is to choose to continue to love throughout the years.

Two great friends, Bill Hewlett and David Packard, built one of the great American corporations—Hewlett-Packard. Bill and David met as freshmen at Stanford University and maintained their friendship for almost 70 years until David's death. Throughout the years of their friendship their trust for each other continued to grow. There is no record that the two of them ever had a fight.[8] Rather than letting the pressure of being in business together pull them apart, they remained open and receptive to each other. "Because they trusted each other completely, they could trust their employees, their customers, even their competitors."[9] Theirs was a large-hearted friendship.

The investment of large-heartedness helps sustain and deepen long-term friendships. Large-heartedness provides a fertile field in which the friendship can grow. Long-term friendships are one of the great experiences of a lifetime. Time cannot destroy them, distance cannot prevent them, and death cannot silence them. Long-term friendships are secured in your heart and mind over time. Your love for and memory of your friend only grows in strength as time passes. This sort of friendship is truly a powerful thing.

Stronger Than Time, Distance or Death
The Long-term Effect of Great Friendships

Having considered the encouragement and investment that are at the core of great friendships, it is easy to imagine the long-term effects of such relationships. First of all, long-term friendships help us learn important lessons about long-term commitments that aren't required, but that are freely made. Secondly, in great friendships we have friends who know our history and whose advice comes with an awareness of who we are and where we've been. This gives their advice great value. Finally, those who have been great friends through the years have helped us to gain the courage to become the persons that we were meant to be. To summarize, the long-term effect of great friendships is that in them we experience loyalty, understanding, and courage.

So, what does this have to do with lifestyle leadership? A great deal. As leaders it is extremely important that we give loyalty, understanding, and courage to those we lead. It is also important that we motivate them to give the same to others on the team and to those that they will lead in the future. Where do we learn about loyalty, understanding, and courage, learning both what they look like and how to give them? One great place to learn about and experience them is in great friendships. The long-term effect is powerful.

The Message to Your Children

Parents are constantly perplexed in knowing how to teach their children to treat their friends right. Perhaps we should do less teaching and provide more demonstration. Our kids learn how to treat their friends by watching how we treat our friends. If we have no friends, we teach our kids that friends are either not important or are something for which you will eventually outgrow your need. We reproduce our isolation in them. If we have friendships that are largely superficial and self-serving, we teach our kids that friendship is about insincerity and selfishness.

If we have friendships that are based upon encouragement and investments, then we teach our kids that friendships are about loyalty, understanding, and courage. Indirectly, we also teach them that friendships are important, that we never outgrow our need for friends, and that true friendships require sincerity and selflessness. In leading our children it is important that we lead them in building good friendships. As is true with all great leadership, we must lead them to do as we do, not just do what we say.

The Compounding Benefit of Lifelong Friendships

With the power of compounding interest, a small investment over time can become a great amount of money. This is especially true if you continue to invest throughout the years. Lifelong friendships have similar compounding benefits. A small investment in a friendship in the beginning that is added throughout the years becomes a great treasure. The loyalty, understanding, and courage only increase in value as the years advance.

In the opening story you read about the last conversation between John and Ken before John's death. This story is based upon my last conversation with a dear friend named John who died in his late thirties as a result of colon cancer. I met John when we were in college and was his friend for almost twenty years. Through our friendship, we both learned important lessons about loyalty, understanding, and courage. And although he has been deceased for a number of years, those lessons remain strong in my heart and mind. Whenever I think of him or visit his grave, there really is only one thing I know to say; it is the only thing that needs to be said: "Thank you."

Lifestyle leaders need great friends. You will find great friends as you become a great friend. And remember again:

Two are better than one, because they have a good return for their work:
If one falls down, his friend can help him up.
But pity the man who falls and has no one to help him up!
Also, if two lie down together, they will keep warm. But how can one keep warm alone?
Though one may be overpowered, two can defend themselves.
A cord of three strands is not quickly broken.[10]

10 · A Harvest of Goodness

The Fruit of a Life of Influence

Fran wiped the tear from her eye and Joe cleared his throat as the last of their kids and grandkids drove away. They walked back into the quietness of their home, holding hands and turned their attention to the boxes and thought: "What are we going to do with those things?"

Fran and Joe's birthdays were eight days apart, and all of the kids and grandchildren had come to celebrate their 81st birthdays. The home that now seemed so large was bursting at the seams with the addition of their three children, their children's spouses, and the grandkids. Regardless of the chaos, it had been a great weekend. When the birthday presents were brought out, Fran and Joe had had no idea what could be in the one huge box and the other small box.

Fran and Joe had opened the gifts together, slowly tearing away the festive paper. Inside the larger box sat a brand new, top-of-the-line computer, monitor, and printer. The small box contained a micro-cassette tape recorder. These gifts came with the following instructions:

Mom and Dad:

Almost everything we know about life we learned from you. Our days now are so filled with busyness that we feel we are forgetting the many things that you taught us. We don't want to forget the lessons from your lives. We want to live them out with our spouses and teach them to our kids. So again, as has been true all along, we need your help.

Please take this computer and tape recorder and tell us again the things that you have already taught us. Please focus on those things that long after you are gone you want us to remember and to pass on to our children.

We know this will take time and there may be some early frustration in learning to use this new computer. Be that as it may, we remind you of what you always taught us: "Great leaders are great servants." Please lead us one more time.

With all of our love and appreciation,
Meredith, Abby, and Jon

Sitting down at the dining room table, Fran and Joe looked at each other, then at the computer looming on one end of the table and the tape recorder on the other. Fran spoke first. "Joe," she said, "we can either look at this as a bother and a threat to our comfort zone or as one of our last great opportunities to lead our kids and their kids. I think we need to make the most of this opportunity."

Joe slowly exhaled a long, deep breath, smiled at his wife, and pushed his glasses up on his nose. Looking at the computer, he said, "How did they say you turn this darn thing on?"

Over the subsequent weeks, laughter spilled from the dining room as they worked on their project. Joe had come up with a very broad outline of what they had tried to teach their kids, and Fran was working on the details. As they wrapped up their work on the project one night, Fran looked at Joe and said, "Joe, maybe this project is as much for our benefit as for the kids." Joe knew exactly what she was thinking. "I agree. It's been a long time since I've thought about the many opportunities that we've had over the years to invest in the lives of others. We've been able to plant many seeds into others' lives. I hope that long after we are gone, there will be a great harvest of goodness."

A Heritage of Positive Influence

Lifestyle leaders realize that death comes to all of us. This realization serves as a great reminder that the years of our leadership will come to an end. For most of us, our lives will pass far more quickly than we could have ever imagined. If we have invested our lives and gifts in others, we will leave behind a harvest and a heritage that continues after we are gone from this life. Those good things that we have planted in the lives of others will multiply into a great harvest of goodness that is far more abundant than the few seeds that we planted.

The heritage that we want to leave behind for our spouses, children, coworkers, and neighbors includes four gifts of positive influence based in truth and purpose.

Fruitful Lives: The Gifts of Giving and Learning to Give

We show our love for others by giving to them. Our faith, abilities, possessions, expertise, money, time, privileges, and energy are all things that can bless the lives of others. We want our lives and leadership to be a reminder to others of the importance of giving; by giving freely, we can inspire those around us to give.

It is important that we not only give to others, but that we also help them to learn to give. One of the great gifts we can leave behind for others is an appreciation of the value of giving. In giving to others we hope to teach them that a fruitful life is not about acquiring and keeping. It is rather about the ability and willingness to give to others. As people remember that which we gave them, it will motivate them to give of what they have to others.

Meaningful Lives: The Gift of Wisdom

Lifestyle leaders continually learn. They value the attainment of practical wisdom and believe that part of what they can give to others is their own life wisdom. They share their wisdom not out of a desire to impress, but rather to help others have meaningful lives. They want to leave behind a tradition of valuing and sharing wisdom that brings greater meaning and purpose to life.

Effective Lives: The Gift of Preparation

Lifestyle leaders anticipate and help meet the developmental needs of others. It is the gift of preparation, which involves helping others get ready for their future leadership challenges. The motivation for giving this gift is our desire to help others be effective in accomplishing the God-given purposes that they have in this life. The hope of this gift is that long after the lifestyle leader is gone, those that they helped will be leading well in their spheres of influence.

Godly Lives: The Gift of Grace

We also need to remember that none of us is smart enough, good enough, strong enough, or positive enough to succeed in life apart from God. Every day of our lives we need His grace to succeed in meeting the day's challenges. We want a strong reminder of the need for God and His grace at the core of our heritage. Our lives should be a simple reminder of the importance of knowing God. Our hope is that in some way, our lives will be a source of grace to those that we influence.

These four gifts are important ones for us to give to others while we have the opportunity to do so. These gifts serve as a heritage that will continue on when our years of influence are over. Hopefully, they will be gifts that keep on giving.

As One Speaking From the Dust
A Life that Blesses Beyond the Grave

Appropriately, it is said of the Biblical character Able that, because of his faithfulness, "...though he is dead, he still speaks."[1] The message of Able's life did not end at the grave. It continues to serve as a reminder to us today of the importance of faithfulness.

As we find purpose in leading out of who we are rather than merely out of the positions that we hold, our lives develop a quality that continues to speak long after we are gone. I knew of an estate attorney who told his client that he could not structure his will in a way that would let him rule from the grave. Once he was dead, his ability to rule over people was dead as well. Our hope as lifestyle leaders is not to rule from the grave. Our hope is that our example of lifestyle leadership will continue to speak to and encourage others long after we are gone. It is our hope that our lives will continue to encourage others to face the challenges inherent to lifestyle leadership. When those we have touched consider the message of our life, we hope it will speak with strength and clarity toward principled leadership.

Stories and Commitments that Light the Way

Public speakers quickly learn that people remember the stories. Lifestyle leaders learn the same lesson. After we are gone, those that we have led will not remember all of the instruction we gave them about leadership. They will remember the ways we exemplified lifestyle leadership in our own lives. It will be the stories from our life that will give light to their paths as they face their leadership challenges.

The commitments our constituents saw us keep, no matter the cost, will also light their paths. Each time we maintain commitments to principles and people, unwilling to compromise our standards, will serve as a bright torch as they wrestle with making and keeping commitments. Our example can give others the courage to make and keep their promises, long after we leave the scene.

In order to leave behind stories and examples of how we kept commitments, we must let people get close enough to truly see us. As we lead them, we must engage personally and mindfully with them; it is this sort of involvement that allows stories and examples to naturally develop. We want our leadership to "rub off" on as many people as possible. This direct engagement requires close interaction over time. It also requires vulnerability. It is through this kind of interaction that stories are transmitted, stories that will continue to speak long after we are gone. When we can leave compelling stories and examples behind us, we have a sense that our stewardship of lifestyle leadership is complete.

A Stewardship Completed

A steward is someone who has been given a charge or responsibility to fulfill. Our stewardship is the charge or responsibility that we have been given to fulfill. When we die, we want to have fully completed our responsibility to provide lifestyle leadership to those in our spheres of influence. We will not have fulfilled our charge perfectly; there will be no room for arrogance. But there can be the reality that we have led others to the best of our abilities, in a way that flows out of who we are and not just out of the titles we hold. And when we failed to lead as we should, we can take comfort in the knowledge that we took responsibility for our shortcomings and made things right to the best of our abilities.

But who gave us this stewardship? I believe that our stewardship has three sources. First, the people who selected us for leadership positions. We certainly have responsibilities to keep to them. Second, those who by following us empowered us. The stakeholders who empowered us by believing in us and helping us along the way fall into this second group. These people gave us their trust and their belief, and we are accountable to them to fulfill our stewardship.

Third, and the most important, source for our stewardship is God. I believe that God is the ultimate source of our stewardship. As we come to know Him and develop our relationship with Him, we also come to more clearly understand the stewardship for lifestyle leadership that He has for each of us. There is a dimension to our leadership that we can never fully understand and never fully complete apart from our understanding and right relationship with God. He has a charge for us to fulfill in this life, and we cannot understand that charge or fulfill it apart from Him.

By faithfully fulfilling our stewardship of lifestyle leadership, we are able to die with a clear conscience toward those we led. A successful lifestyle leader can look back upon his or her life and say: "I did the best that I could to lead. When I failed in my efforts, I took responsibility for my actions. I was not perfect, but I did consistently choose to live the life and exert the leadership required of a lifestyle leader." People who can look back at their lives with this sort of vision can also die with a clear conscience toward those who gave us the responsibility to lead. We have fulfilled the charge that they entrusted to us.

A Life of Integrity and Blessing, Built One Day at a Time

Most significant achievements are built one day and step at a time. This is certainly true with the achievement of lifestyle leadership. The following four daily steps will move us forward in the adventure of lifestyle leadership.

Daily Decisions for Integrity and Balance

Every day, we must choose to align our character, competence, and commitment with our core beliefs and virtues. To the degree that these three components of our leadership are aligned with and drawn from our core beliefs and virtue, to that degree we lead with integrity. It is a daily discipline to take a few minutes to assess if we are leading with integrity. It should also be a regular discipline to gain outside perspective on the integrity of our leadership.

There is also the daily decision to faithfully manage the conflicting demands of our various responsibilities. As we discussed in Chapter One, each of these responsibility areas is important and each has to work. Each day, we take steps forward in our journey of lifestyle leadership as we manage well the conflicting demands of our lives, and thereby work toward balance.

Daily Quest for Humility and Boldness

Arrogance and lifestyle leadership are mutually exclusive terms. Lifestyle leaders realize that at best they are fulfilling a stewardship with which they have been entrusted. They must work toward success in accomplishing their stewardship. When they succeed, they must lay that success at the feet of those who entrusted the stewardship to them. Lifestyle leadership is not about proving or defining ourselves. It should at every point be about humble service.

A leader's humility should not divert him/her away from bold action. A leader's humility ought rather to give her a basis for bold action that rises above ego and control. I understand boldness to mean instant principled action. Lifestyle leaders must make the daily choice of decisive action that is derived from a clear and principled understanding of her context and responsibilities. Our humility gives us a basis for boldness. Our boldness is essential in accomplishing with humility the stewardship with which we have been entrusted.

Daily Commitment to Serve and Invest

In his book, *Leadership Is an Art*, Max DePree challenges leaders: "The first responsibility of a leader is to define reality. The last is to say thank you. In between the two, the leader must become a servant and a debtor."[2]

Obviously, DePree believes that much of leadership is servanthood. This is not to be understood as bowing to the whims of those we lead. That would neither be servanthood nor leadership. Servanthood in this context means that we serve those we lead by helping them accomplish the mission, vision and values of the organization, and as is possible, by helping them succeed at life. We work toward mastering ourselves so that we may serve others.

We also have the daily choice and privilege of investing in those we lead. This investing will occur in small daily choices that we make to lend our time, expertise, resources, and attention to meet the developmental needs of our followers. Each day we want to invest purposefully and discerningly into the lives of those that we lead. In so doing, we serve them well, using all that we have to help them move forward in their growth and development.

Daily Focus on Significant Accomplishment

Lifestyle leaders understand the simple test of leadership. The test consists of three questions:

1. What specific people am I leading?
2. What exactly am I leading them to do or to become?
3. Are they doing it or becoming it?

These questions bring us down from the clouds of leadership musings and focus us on the context in which today we must work toward significant accomplishment. The adage goes that *he who leads and no one follows is merely taking a walk*. Leaders take walks when they fail to focus on leading specific people toward the accomplishment of specific goals. It is easy to dwell on our knowledge of leadership and on our ethical treatment of others. These are essential ingredients to lifestyle leadership. They are deficient unless they are linked with regular, significant accomplishments that move toward the achievement of the organization's mission, vision and values.

The seven leadership competencies mentioned in Chapter 3 should serve as a regular assessment tool for lifestyle leaders. These competencies are a certain guide in determining how to lead others to attain significant accomplishments. They also serve as a reminder to us to flex our leadership so that we practice all seven competencies and not just the ones with which we feel most comfortable. Practicing the competencies helps us to maintain a daily focus on significant accomplishment.

Daily Need for Grace, Love, and Forgiveness

Each of us has a daily need for grace, love, and forgiveness. We need grace, which is underserved kindness, help, or favor, because we are never fully able to be and to do what we know we ought to be and do. We need the help that we do not always deserve. There is in us the daily need for grace.

We also have the need for daily love, to know that someone cares and is committed to us. We need the strength and motivation that comes from knowing that we are loved unconditionally. Part of great leadership is that over time you come to love those that you lead. It is very difficult to have enduring love for others unless we ourselves are loved. Each day we need to be engaged in those right relationships in which we are loved, and to work in those relationships to clear away conflicts that block love.

Each of us also has a daily need for forgiveness. As leaders, we will make wrong choices. Moreover, as humans we realize that there is in each of us a dark twisted nature that loves wrong and hates right. We need forgiveness for doing wrong and for being wrong. In believing this, I do not see humanity as only being inherently wrong or malevolent. I see us rather as good people who have deep brokenness inside that enables wrong actions outside. For this reason, we are in daily need for forgiveness.

If we ignore and repress this need for daily grace, love, and forgiveness, we will increasingly diminish our humanity. These needs are part of what it means to be human. By ignoring and repressing these needs, part of who we are dies. We also must not manipulate those that we lead to meet this need for grace, love, and forgiveness. When we manipulate others to meet our personal needs, we abandon leadership. Our focus shifts from our people and from the mission, vision, and values of the organization to ourselves, and our leadership falters.

I believe that some of our need for daily grace, love, and forgiveness will be met through our right relationships with others. However, ultimately these needs must be met through our relationship with God. When we have been graced, loved, and forgiven by Him, we rebuild our supply of these important gifts to give to others, and we find our own need for these three things is being satisfied. Part of what keeps us involved in the challenge of great leadership is the daily decision to find the grace, love, and forgiveness for which we long.

One day those you led will remember your life and leadership. You may be fortunate enough to be asked to write down the heritage that you want to leave behind, as Fran and Joe were in our opening story. All of us are recording the heritage we will leave behind in the hearts and minds of those that we lead. It is my hope that by God's grace your life will provide wonderful memories of great leadership to many people, and that when you depart this life you will leave behind a great harvest of goodness. I wish you God's blessings as you move forward in the great adventure of lifestyle leadership.

Notes

Chapter 1

[1] Associated Press News Report, November 23, 1996.

[2] Stephen Covey, *Principle-Centered Leadership*, Fireside Book, 1990, and Ken Blanchard and Sheldon Bowles, *Gung Ho!*, William Morrow and Company, Inc., 1998.

[3] *Character First*, Institute in Basic Life Principles, Oak Brook, Illinois.

Chapter 2

[1] Davenport, Thomas. "The Fad that Forgot People," *Fast Company*, November 1995, http://www.fastcompany.com/online/01/reengin.html.

[2] "Champy's Prescription: Reengineer Thyself," *Chemical Week*, February 16, 1995.

[3] White, Randall P., Hodgson, Philip and Crainer, Stuart, *The Future of Leadership*, Pitman Publishing, 1996, p. 16.

[4] Singer, Jennifer. "Generation E," *Home Office Computing*, December 1995, p. 54.

[5] Lane, Randall. "Computers are Our Friends," *Forbes Magazine*, May 8, 1995, p. 102.
[6] "Landry Is Lauded," *The New York Times*, February 18, 2000, p. 8.
[7] "Landry Is Lauded," p. 8.
[8] Duck, Jeanie Daniel, "Managing Change: The Art of Balance," *Harvard Business Review*, November-December 1993, re printed in *Wellcome News*, Burroughs Wellcome Company, August-September 1994, p. 12.
[9] Drucker, Peter F. *Managing for the Future*, Truman Talley Books, 1992, p. 122.

Chapter 3

[1] Edward R. Murrow in May 1963 in a testimony before a US Congress Congressional Committee.
[2] *Principle-Centered Leadership*, Stephen Covey, p. 31.
[3] In a speech entitled *Leadership and Moral Purpose* given by Max De Pree as the Leon I. Gintzig Commemorative Lecture at the American College of Healthcare Executives Congress on Administration, March 1993.
[4] "Managing Change: The Art of Balancing," Jeanie Daniel Duck, *Harvard Business Review*, November-December 1993.
[5] *Empires of the Mind*, Denis Waitley, p. 15.

Chapter 4

[1] Proverbs 27:6
[2] Gertrude Himmelfarb, The Demoralization of Society, Vintage Books, 1996, p. 11.
[3] Himmelfarb, pages 12-13.

Chapter 5

[1] Proverbs 16:25
[2] Proverbs 13:10, 20
[3] Handy, Charles, *The Hungry Spirit*, New York: Broadway Books, 1998, p. 78.
[4] Handy, p. 78.
[5] Schaeffer, Francis A., *How Should We Then Live*, Old Tappan, New Jersey: Fleming H. Revell Company, 1976, pp. 71-73.
[6] Psalms 62:5-7
[7] Jeremiah 29:13-14

Chapter 6

[1] *Marriages Go Begging for Care As Focus Turns to Kids, Jobs*, Sue Shellenbarger, The Wall Street Journal Interactive Edition, December 24, 1997.
[2] Crabb, Lawrence J., *The Marriage Builder*, Grand Rapids, Michigan: Zondervan Publishing, 1982, pp. 31-32.
[3] I Corinthians 13:4-8.

Chapter 7

1 *Teen Ethics: More Cheating and Lying*, Karen Thomas, USA Today, October 18, 1998, Vol. 17, Issue 25, p. 1D.
2 *Teen Ethics: More Cheating and Lying*, p. 1D.
3 *Teen Ethics: More Cheating and Lying*, p. 1D.
4 Titus, Dale N., *Values Education in American Secondary Schools*, A paper presented at the Kutztown University Education Conference, Kutztown, PA, September 16, 1994.
5 Maddi, S.R. and Kobasa, S.C., *The Hardy Executive: Health Under Stress*, Chicago: Dorsey Professional Books/Dow Jones–Irwin, 1984, pp. 31-32.
6 Kouzes, James M. and Barry Z. Posner, *The Leadership Challenge*, San Francisco: Jossey-Bass Publishers, 1995, p. 72.
7 Kouzes, James M. and Barry Z. Posner, *The Leadership Challenge*, San Francisco: Jossey-Bass Publishers, 1995, p. 73.

Chapter 8

1 Havel, Vaclav, *Disturbing the Peace: A Conversation with Karel Hvizdala*, trans. Paul Wilson, New York: Vintage Books, 1990, p. 72.
2 Frost, Robert, *Mountain Interval*, New York: Henry Holt and Company, 1920, Bartleby.com, 1999, www.bartleby.com/119/, October 5, 2000.

3 Covey, Stephen R., *Principle-Centered Leadership*, New York: Fireside Books, 1990, p. 14.
4 Kouzes, James M. and Barry Z. Posner, *The Leadership Challenge*, San Francisco: Jossey-Bass Publishers, 1995, pp. 325-326.
5 Kouzes, James M. and Barry Z. Posner, *The Leadership Challenge*, p. 325.
6 Twain, Mark, *Puddn'head Wilson's Calendar*.
7 DePree, Max, *Leadership Is an Art*, New York: Dell Publishing, 1989, p. 70.

Chapter 9

1 Eccl. 4:9-12 *The New International Version*, (Grand Rapids, MI: Zondervan Publishing House) 1984.
2 Nancy Ann Jeffrey, "Whatever Happened to Friendship," *Wall Street Journal*, 3 March 2000, W1.
3 Carol Hymowitz, "New Top Managers Often Find They Miss Close Peers," Counsel, *Wall Street Journal*, 25 November 1997, B1.
4 Proverbs 27:17 *The New International Version*, (Grand Rapids, MI: Zondervan Publishing House) 1984.
5 Eccl. 4:13, *The New Revised Standard Version*, (Nashville, TN: Thomas Nelson Publishers) 1989.
6 *Merriam-Webster's Collegiate Dictionary*, 10th ed., s.v. "courage."
7 Noel M. Tichy and Stratford Sherman, "Control Your Destiny Or Someone Else Will," *Harper Business* (1994): 15.

[8] Michael S. Malone, "The Soul of the 'HP Way,'" *Wall Street Journal*, 16 January, 2001, A26.
[9] Michael S. Malone, "The Soul of the 'HP Way,'" *Wall Street Journal*, 16 January, 2001, A26.
[10] Eccl. 4:9-12 *The New International Version*, (Grand Rapids, MI: Zondervan Publishing House) 1984.

Chapter 10

[1] The Epistle to the Hebrews 11:4.

About the Author

"In its essence, leadership is a lifestyle, not a position."

 John Hawkins, president and founder of Leadership Edge Incorporated, specializes in helping current and emerging business leaders wrestle with the issue of developing their leadership lifestyle. He believes that this is essential for effective, long-term leadership in today's chaotic organizations and corporations.

Providing seminars and presentations for corporations such as *American Express, Blue Cross Blue Shield, The U.S. Department of Commerce,* and *Glaxo Wellcome Pharmaceuticals,* John stays in touch with the demands on leaders in organizations today. For the Leadership Edge bi-monthly newsletter, *Positive Impact,* John researches and writes thoughtful and practical applications for principled leadership.

John is a 1998 graduate of the Harvard University Master Class for Leadership Educators at the Kennedy School of Government. As a founding member of the Duke University Interfraternity Council Board of Advisors, John designed and facilitated leadership development programs for the Duke fraternity system. In the Spring of 2000, John was awarded the *William J.*

Maschke Award for the excellence of his leadership development programs.

John has been published in numerous journals and publications including: *Executive Excellence, Personal Excellence, The New York Times, Bottom Line Business, Student Leader Magazine, The Journal of the Service Industry Association* and *The Journal of Leadership and Management in Engineering.*

In his videotape, *Winning the Right to Influence,* John shares with managers and leaders a challenging and effective approach to leading and motivating today's entry-level, twenty-something employees. Businesses such as the Southwestern Company and Alcon Laboratories use this 30-minute training tool in their internal employee development programs. John is also a qualified trainer for Ken Blanchard's Situational Leadership® II training program.

Above his career success, John is most proud of his 24-year marriage to his wife, Janet, and of their three children: Laura, Gary, and Will. In their family, John has learned the most practical lessons on leadership.

John Hawkins
Leadership Lifestyle
PO Box 51685
Durham, NC 27717
919-493-6607
jhawkins@leadershiplifestyle.com
www.leadershiplifestyle.com

Other Books on Leadership
from Executive Excellence Publishing

 **Leadership from the Inside Out**
Kevin Cashman

Discover a whole-person approach to leadership that reminds us that the ability to grow as a leader is based on the ability to grow as a person. The journey of self and leadership development focuses on seven major pathways to mastery in a multidimensional and interdisciplinary manner.

Paperback **$15.95**

 **The Spirit of Leadership**
Robert J. Spitzer

This book probes deeply into all the major roots of organzational spirit, such as ethics, credibility, widom, fair conduct, charisma, self-examination, comtemplation, committment, and purpose.

Hardcover **$24.95**

 **A New Paradigm of Leadership**
Ken Shelton, editor

This compilation offers fresh perspectives on leadership from top CEOs and consultants, who answer questions like: How can leaders make the transition to the new paradigm of continuous change and increased flexibility? How can leaders form partnerships with their employees that allow for increased teamwork, bolder decisions, and performance-based pay while maintaining the balance between growth and profitability?

Hardcover **$20.00**

 **Integrity at Work**
Ken Shelton, editor

Managers face difficult moral and ethical dilemmas. This compilation features over 50 executives and consultants who have made high ethical standards and honest business practices a top priority in their organizations. These leaders share their views on fostering honest behavior, dealing with ethical dilemmas, and leading by moral example.

Hardcover **$20.00**